Net Gains

C000128062

Net Gains

A guide to ministry

Andrew Pratt

Copyright © Andrew Pratt 2008

Cover image © PureStockX

Scripture Quotations are from the New Revised Standard Version of the Bible, (Anglicized Edition) © 1989, 1995 by the Division of Christian Education of the National Council of the Churches of Christ in the United States of America. Used by permission. All rights reserved.

British Library Cataloguing in Publication data
A catalogue record for this book is available
from the British Library

ISBN 978-1-905958-20-7

First published by Inspire
4 John Wesley Road
Werrington
Peterborough PE4 6ZP

Printed and bound in Great Britain by
Athenaeum Press Ltd, Gateshead, Tyne & Wear

Contents

Introduction
How to use this book

If you are reading this book you may already be an ordained minister or someone preparing for ordination. Equally you may be involved in lay ministry or working beside and supporting others involved in specific ministries. Whatever your role, you will still be willing to learn.

This book is intended to be practical. In one sense, any minister could have written it. It is based on experience and the stories woven into it are real. You can read right through it or just go to the chapter you need. While there is a theological basis, the main intention is to enable those who are preparing for ministry or already involved in it to follow their calling more effectively than they are doing now.

Throughout the text there are poems and hymns. These are my own personal reflections. Read them if it helps. They can provide an oasis or a jumping-off point for your own reflection as the book progresses.

At the end of each chapter are further suggestions for action in the form of a summary of important points from the chapter and thoughts to take things further. The latter are not instant fixes. Some may set an agenda for the whole of your ministry or the rest of your life. Others may be related to a specific task or situation. In all instances, they are there to help us, you and me, grow into the ministry to which we feel called.

God bless you as you go and God go with you. There is excitement ahead.

Note and Acknowledgements

Perhaps you wonder about the title of this book, *Net Gains*. Before entering the ministry I trained as a marine biologist. The allusion to fishing and 'fishers of men' in the Bible amuses me and so 'net gains'. A a poet I enjoy puns so perhaps this also has something to say about the net gain, what's left of the Church, of God's work, by the time we're finished. Whatever you make of it, much of this book is based on over 20 years of experience in Methodist ministry. Inevitably when you draw on experience, real events come to mind, but I have changed names and altered details to preserve people's anonymity.

I am grateful to all those who have made this book possible, those who have tutored me, colleagues, students and countless people with whom I have shared ministry over the years. Thank you.

Net Gains was written during a sabbatical enabled by the Methodist Church, during which I was able to reflect on my work as tutor at Luther King House, living and learning with people exploring vocation and preparing for ministry. Two colleagues, John Harrod and Jane Craske, took an extra burden of work at this time. My thanks are particularly due to them.

Chapter 1
What on earth are you doing?

What's God got to do with it?

In the beginning: God. Come back to that again and again. Were it not for God, you would not be reading this book because you would not have been called to ministry or be working with people who have been. Were it not for a sense of vocation, God's call, I would not have survived this far in ministry and I wouldn't be writing this.

> Now wherever God's own presence
> breaks into our common ground,
> on the mountain, in the temple,
> loudly, or without a sound,
> there the vision that God offers
> challenges all we have found.
>
> Here a different way is offered,
> now a fresh resolve is framed,
> as the servants of the servant
> find that even they are named;
> and the call of God is echoed
> as each new found life is claimed.*

Ministry is partly being and partly doing. Trying to disentangle the two is impossible. A friend of mine was once a policeman. Now, ministry is not just a job, but there's something here we can learn. Bob has long since retired from the force, but there is something that makes me still feel that he is a policeman. It changes the way I respond to him. Similarly, those who act as ministers, representatives of the Church, set apart in one way or another, ordained or not, have a different character. God seems to invest something in them irrespective of their own theology or understanding, regardless of what they do, what their function is. Their way of being is different.

Sometimes the only way we can minister is through our being. There are no words, no actions, nothing to be done. God simply commands our presence – in worship, with those who mourn, in celebration, beside those serving tea, in the sacramental but also in the mundane.

A lot of ministry can look like social work to the outsider, and in many ways it is, but, if that is the limit of it, then something vital is missing that ought to

* Andrew Pratt. Reproduced by permission of Stainer & Bell Ltd.

3

inform all we do and all we are. God has everything to do with ministry, and ministry has everything to do with God.

People

If ministry is nothing without God, it is equally true that ministry is always about people. It inevitably has a pastoral element. If it doesn't, you're missing something. That is true whatever your theology. I remember, years ago, learning about the priesthood of Moses. It was used as a model for all priesthood. Moses, it was said, represented God to the people and the people to God. Moses was also a prophet calling people back to God. In each role, whatever our view of God, Moses had a relationship with people.

For some this harks too far back in history. They would argue that there is a sharp demarcation between the Old and New Testaments. Jesus supersedes all that has been before. He becomes the model for our ministry. That all seems very straightforward – until we reflect on it a bit. Think on this:

> Jesus was dedicated in a temple, came of age with a Jewish bar mitzvah and was baptized as an adult. There is no record of him being married and he was buried in a borrowed grave with, as far as we can see, no funeral service. As far as the gospel record indicates he baptized no one (in spite of the 'Great Commission'), married no one and when called to minister to the bereaved raised the dead!

You still think that you can base your ministry on that of Jesus? It is not as simple as all that, which is why I want to come down to a pattern for ministry that is rooted and grounded in God, yet altogether human.

It is a tangled web we weave

Ministry is about relationships and, whatever we think of God or Jesus, when we minister, we deal with people – real people, with all their problems and foibles and fears. A poem might throw this into focus:

> I long to grieve with all my heart,
> he was the closest one to me;
> but there is one who takes my place,
> it is her grief the world will see.

> Within the coldness of my room
> I tear at pillows, scream inside.
> Beyond these walls I wear a mask
> while others point, and some deride.

They do not understand, the love
that held us through the winter's gloom,
that painted colours in the spring,
that now I share an empty room.

O Lord you understood the one
who drew you water from a well.
You recognised her chequered life,
but offered love instead of hell.

I'm trapped and yet the love we shared
held beauty and was meant to be.
O God, am I entirely wrong?
O hold me fast and comfort me.*

I wonder how you react to these words. Who are they about? What story do they tell? To begin with, there are three people in the first verse. Things are not straightforward. There is grief. There has been a death. The person speaking feels displaced. Out of natural human curiosity, we begin to ask questions. Was she divorced or the mistress of the man who has died? Imagine that she has come to you for support. Where do you begin and how do you feel?

Let me add another layer to the story. Suppose that you have been involved with the man and woman, that you have ministered to the widow. Now how do you react to the one who also longs to grieve with all her heart?

Imagine you have known the couple for some years. They seemed to be happily married, but you have to admit you only really knew their public faces. Let me fill you in on a few things.

I'll begin with Jim. Jim you knew as a steward in your church. He seemed to command respect. He was well organized, helpful, considerate. He had a responsible job in commerce. He and his wife were comfortably off. When he was a child, Jim was not particularly strong. Often he was bullied at school. When he got home, his father would tell him that he should give as good as he got, try to 'teach him a lesson'. A man who had a gentle exterior, Jim's father was brutal at home. Jim had seen his mother beaten more times than he wanted to remember. This had been a learning ground for him, a time when his character had been formed. His relationships with women always began gently enough, but soon deteriorated into control and often physical violence.

Jane, Jim's wife, did not see that side of his character until a couple of years into their marriage. She was an easy-going woman who kept close to his side and never did anything that was likely 'to set him off', as she later recalled. Gradually, she had seen how the land lay. She would spend more and

---

* Andrew Pratt. Reproduced by permission of Stainer & Bell Ltd.

more time at work and Jim had more and more freedom. She regretted 'neglecting' him.

Christine had been on her own for many years. Strong and independent, she had met Jim through work, found him charming and quite humorous, a man of the world. She also went to church, but a different denomination. They had enough in common to provide enjoyable conversation. He filled a gap in her life and experience and he found a bit of excitement with her that seemed to be lacking with his wife. Christine had yet to experience Jim's rougher side. Then she heard from a friend of his death. She didn't know that he was married – she had felt that *she* was likely to become his wife; he had implied that, or so she thought. His death was sudden – a heart attack brought on by stress the coroner said.

It is into this situation that you have been called. Christine contacted you as Jim's friend. You were a minister to Christine and Jim. Nothing is straightforward.

Tangled up in our pastoral relationships are our own feelings and background and that prophetic strand which asks the questions, 'Where is God in all of this? What would God say or do?' It is tempting to play God, to 'magnify his strictures with a zeal he would not own', as the hymnwriter Frederick Faber would say. The next question for you in this situation is, 'Is it legitimate for me to minister to someone who might, in the eyes of the world, be in the wrong?'

It is at this point that we need to reflect theologically, which can be quite a simple process. Jesus met a woman at a well who needed his care. He approached her, took the initiative, asked for a drink, joined her in conversation. From the point of view of the world and his faith, he shouldn't even have spoken to her. So, the door is open for us to make contact with all people, but we need to know how we feel and where we stand before we do. Remember, whoever you are speaking to is a human being, someone loved by God. Of course that is true of the other people in the story, too, and, as the minister, you would be dealing with them all. It's quite a tangle.

Well, things are not always this simple! What if the three people were all men or all women. Now how do you feel? Does your attitude change?

Pastorally, there are always questions of an obvious, relatively simple nature. Overlaying these are our own backgrounds and experience. We bring our own prejudices to every conversation, whether we like it or not, and we have to live with the words we say, the decisions we make and the wounds we cause. So do the people we're dealing with. We have to be true to our own integrity and we need to know what that means. Otherwise, we end up playing games with people's lives and making hypocrites of ourselves. Hypocrites were the only people Jesus consistently and roundly condemned.

In the context of the story, we need to know where we stand in relation to divorce, adultery and domestic violence or, in the case of second interpretation, how we cope with gay and lesbian relationships. If our views mean that we cannot do anything other than condemn, then we'd better not do anything.

One thing is sure, people coming to Jesus, other than hypocrites, went away from him feeling better for the meeting. We should seek to enable the same sense of healing. Broaden your thoughts out beyond this one poem, this single story, and you have a rule of thumb that you can apply to all pastoral relationships. The end goal of these or any other encounters is to leave each and every person you are ministering to better than you found them. The process of ministry is to heal and help. If our own prejudices in any situation prevent us from doing our best to achieve these ends, then we need to let someone else do the ministering. To do so is not an expression of failure, but an admission that we cannot be all things to all people. We are human, too.

> Why did I do that?
> A question worth asking.
> And where is God in what I'm doing?
> And what could I have done differently?

Going home

Humanity is critical. Jesus told people to love others as they loved themselves. It has been said before, but cannot be said often enough, that we are each worthy of love. We should value ourselves. God has called us with a purpose. We matter.

Coming away from a typical day in ministry, which may have involved sharing heartache and elation, birth and death, sadness and hope, what do we do with our feelings? Some of what we hear – and share, unless we are very insensitive – will touch us profoundly, leave us drained and, sometimes, make sleep difficult. If you live alone, you risk carrying that burden from day to day, week to week, month to month. If you have a partner, he or she is not the most appropriate person with whom to share, with whom to unload. A colleague with whom you can debrief at the end of each day is probably an impossible luxury for most people, but great if you have that sort of support. Some turn to alcohol or drugs, neither of which are recommended, obviously. Still others find solace in illicit relationships – again, not appropriate. The fact remains, though, that we all need support and care, some way of coming home. Those who rely on prayer may find that, in time, they need real human contact, even if at a distance, to mediate God's love and remind them that they still matter, are still of value. This affirmation is not a luxury; it is an essential.

Supervision

As we minister, we are not always the best people to monitor what we are doing. Historically, especially in the free churches, ministry has often been a solitary business. It is easy to excuse our isolation under the guise of a need for confidentiality. Let me give you an example.

The telephone rang. On the other end was a woman. I knew her and her husband. She needed to come round to talk and it seemed urgent. She was not someone to make a fuss, so I suggested that she come right away. It transpired that her marriage was breaking up and she had to share it with someone. She didn't want her husband to know. She talked about everything in confidence.

An hour after she left, the phone rang again. This time it was her husband. Within a short while we were sitting drinking coffee and I was hearing his side of the story. He didn't want his wife to know he'd been – it all had to be in strictest confidence.

To break the trust of either of these people would have been to destroy the pastoral relationship and make it impossible to offer any further help to either of them. The confidence was not broken. The secrets were kept. Had I done the right thing? Had I offered the correct advice, listened in an appropriate way?

The answer is that I had no way of knowing. It certainly wasn't appropriate to share this with my partner. It would have been helpful to have had some advice from someone more experienced, someone outside the pastoral relationship. That needn't have broken the confidence, but, even if my superior could have helped, the structures were not there to facilitate that. Where could I have gone?

If your denomination uses supervision to enable you to reflect on the pastoral care you are trying to offer, then use it. In the same way that a social care professional would do this as a matter of course, so we ought to try to get a second opinion from someone we respect who can be honestly, yet supportively, critical. If there are no such structures available to you, then it is wise to build them yourself. You might form a network with contemporaries or share with a retired minister who is willing to listen and also impart her or his wisdom. In this you will be supported and you may be prevented from making mistakes that harm both you and others. In those instances when you do your best, yet even you know it is not good enough, you will have someone to offer comfort and support who can assure you that it's worth getting up and starting again. You may not be able to put right what has gone wrong, but you will have gained experience and, hopefully, been guarded against despair or cynicism and bitterness.

Such support can make all the difference and break the cycle of loneliness that can so easily break us. We need to know that we are not on our own and, while we know with our heads that God is with us, we often need human reassurance that it is so – an incarnation of that presence in a colleague or friend.

We are involved in a very privileged occupation. We have a sense of a call from God to which we have responded. Our Church, in one way or another, has affirmed that vocation. We are ministers, lay or ordained, doing God's work with God's people. All we do has a basis in Scripture and we have our model for ministry, not in any simplistic way, in Jesus. Yet, the theology and practice must work hand in hand as equal partners. All the time that we reflect theologically on what we are doing, we must also have practice in mind. There is often a tension between pastoral practice and theology. So, while we reflect theologically, we also need to keep in mind the practicality of who the theology is affecting and how it is being applied.

Throughout this book, I will share thoughts and ideas from practical experience. This will not 'teach you to be a minister', but, rather, I hope, sharpen your understanding of yourself and enable you to avoid some of the mistakes from which my own insight, such as it is, has been derived.

Summary

1. Ministry begins with God.
2. Ministry is about people and their relationships with God.
3. People matter because all people are valuable to God.
4. We need to know our points of prejudice and vulnerability and how they might affect our ability to minister.
5. Theology and practice are immutably linked.
6. Support from others can enhance our ability to minister effectively and is indispensible to our well-being.

Looking ahead

- Try to understand yourself.
- Which people do you approve of?
- Who do you find it easy to condemn?
- What is the essence of your faith?
- In what ways are you prejudiced?
- Who supports you?

Chapter 2
Where am I? The context of ministry

I stood at the door of the church after my first service since leaving ministerial training college. As the people left and began to introduce themselves to me, each added to their name and greeting 'I'm from Bourne' or, alternatively, 'I'm from Station Road'. I knew that the congregation had been formed after the amalgamation of two congregations, but that had been seven years ago. Old associations are important and difficult to lose. I know of two Lancashire towns that trace their rivalry back to the Civil War! The story is told of East Anglian villagers who still maintain that they won't associate with the neighbouring village because 'they didn't tell us when the Vikings were coming'!

All of these stories may make you smile, but they point to the fact that we are products of our history and, however hard a new minister may try to make a congregation live in the present for the future, that history will always be there, sometimes in the background sometimes centre stage. If we understand that history, we can minister much more effectively, so this is where I want to begin. Church history and tradition really do have importance if we are willing to apply them to our own particular context.

Of course, there are some churches that are new and appear to have no history at all. Perhaps they have been planted in a new estate or established in a room above a shop. There is no obvious tradition here into which we can tap. They seem to have sprung up out of nowhere. The people who attend do each have a history, though, and the leader of the congregation will also have had experiences that he or she will bring to the new situation, even if this is unknowingly.

Imagine for a moment someone who has given up on the Salvation Army in his youth and gone on to vandalize churches. In his thirties he found himself in hospital for a minor operation. Passing the time, he thumbed through a Gideon's Bible. Imagine that he then went on to lead a church.

Now imagine another person. Cambridge-educated and a solicitor, she has been asked by the clergy of the local cathedral to see what can be done on a rundown neighbouring estate. Each evening, after leaving work and before going to the estate, she attends Evensong. She has been going to Evensong since her teens. The worship is sung and even the Lord's Prayer is intoned so that no one but the choir joins in.

These two people are likely to bring very different influences to bear and the congregations that they lead will, in some way, be influenced by their likes and prejudices. Every congregation, then, has a history, even if it's only the accumulated histories of its members!

Just one more warning before we go any further. Your predecessor may or may not be a good source of information about the place where you are beginning. Six months before I moved to a new appointment, the then incumbent began sending me the church newsletters. It gave me a feel for the place, which was good. Two months before my arrival, I began to receive information about what he was doing and then what he expected me to do. He was not me, though, and I am not him. While such ice-breaking can help, it can also be controlling, putting constraints on you that could be unhelpful and setting goals that you may not be able to meet. Take such 'help' with a pinch of salt. It may be invaluable, but evaluate it wisely.

Mapping the journey

Before we even arrive in a place, an ordnance survey map of the area can give a picture of the way in which it has grown. There may be a centre of population with surrounding villages, parts of a town or city will have their own names indicating that once they were separate hamlets. Industrial history can be seen in the presence of disused factories or workings or in the indication of railway marshalling yards or old lines. Add to this local histories and information from the Internet and we can begin to build up a picture of the background and experience of people among whom we will be working and ministering. All of this history should be treated carefully. None will be without bias.

Another word of caution is also needed. It may be stating the obvious, but, rather like satellite navigation, if what you are reading says you are in a field but you are standing in a housing estate, believe what you see! An old directory of Liverpool gives a picture of that city in the 1800s. Most of the names are male. The occupations overwhelmingly relate to the sea – Ralph Pearson, anchor-smith; Captain John Perkins; Joseph Rigby, roper. The heritage remains, along with the positive evidence of the commerce and poverty borne on the back of slavery and oppression, but this place is no longer dependent on maritime activity. Magnificent buildings rise alongside scenes of degradation. Many of the docks have closed and some have been adapted to provide expensive apartment blocks and shopping outlets. All this might give a picture of wealth and prosperity. In one street that might be true, but walk to the end, cross the road and you could enter a different world where large, once elegant properties, have become dilapidated and been given over to multiple occupation. Often, regeneration of city centres drives the poor to the margins, as the rich flock to places now labelled 'fashionable'.

More and more, we live in a multicultural setting in which people of different ethnic origins and faiths live alongside one another. In parts of the East End of London, this mix can sometimes be discerned down a single street, where Islamic, African-Caribbean Christian, Asian and Rastafarian nestle side by side. In other places – parts of Manchester, for instance – one side of a road may be predominantly Hindu, the other Muslim. All of this is represented in shops and restaurants, dress and custom. For many, their ethnic origin is historic – they are the third or fourth generation living in this country – yet their ethnicity is still important and sometimes reasserted with greater vigour as they sense a loss of culture and identity. Others have been partly or wholly assimilated into this new environment, but it can be cross-cultural, with influences flowing in both directions. Still others find themselves dislocated – knowing something of the roots of their culture in a different continent, yet living the whole of their lives in a context that is predominantly white and European. The signals they are receiving can be confusing and identity is difficult to define. A local council may celebrate Divali alongside Christmas or ban religious symbolism altogether for fear of offence. The understanding of the nature of ministry and mission in societies with a cultural mix is growing.

Faith works, but how can love be shown
within a world of complex care?
Between each nation, in each town
how can God's love be focused there?

A different language, creed or dress
can build a wall and damage life;
and ignorance or fear of faith
could break our trust and fire our strife.

How can we legislate for peace,
or work for human harmony,
within a world of disparate needs,
maintaining our integrity?

God give us confidence to see
your face in people all around
that, in a world of many faiths,
your seeds of love may find rich ground.

Simply to cross a road in some of our cities can take us from wealth to poverty, from crime to respectability. Naturally, churches and their congregations can reflect these transitions. People from one side of a road may attend one church, while those on the other may never come near it. The reasons may be steeped in history, grounded in prejudice or practice, may have profound sociological causes or simply be a matter of preference. Finding out what is going on to cause these invisible barriers can make ministry both easier and more effective.

In summary, it is helpful to know something of the history of an area, but this must be overlaid with observations of the present, our own observations. A period of a year is short enough to move deprivation from one place to another, import prosperity and change the nature of the cityscape in unrecognizable ways. While an overview is helpful, single streets or estates may have a character and nature of their own. We need to use our eyes, ears and brains to judge what is going on in order to temper our ministry so that it meets the needs of those with whom we minister. It is certainly not a case of one sort fits all. It is here that congregational forms of ecclesiology can be most responsive and effective.

How else can we tap into this history? Alongside the sources already mentioned, one of the most important is the people themselves. Sometimes what they provide can be quite formal. One congregation with which I ministered had two local historians, both of whom had written books. One had a lifelong passion for cricket, the other simply liked research. Both wrote well, but each history had a slant to it, a bias. Only by recognizing the bias was it possible to get the most out of each book.

Indeed, in any history we must be aware of bias, which can range from personal or political opinion through to accounts that are pure imagination. A few years ago, a well-known film star wrote a series of books purporting to be biographical. Reading them gave insight into the period in which he had grown up and lived. Any temptation to treat the story of his life as accurate was undermined when a biography was published not long after his death. The actor had been a very private person and wanted to keep it that way, so much of the 'biography' he had written was made up. He was a very good storyteller!

We cannot just read books, still less Internet articles, without applying some intelligent criticism to what we are reading. Be careful is the maxim.

Yet another man I knew wrote about his time in the forces during the war for the benefit of his family. To read his intensely personal account was fascinating. It gave me an insight into him that I would not otherwise have had. It told me something of the relationship he had with his family and the context that had moulded his younger life. The personal nature of the account was both a help and a hindrance. I needed to realize that, if I was drawing my picture of his community from what he had written, I was seeing it through just one person's eyes.

It is not only what people write that can be useful in creating understanding. Privilege is an overused word, but ministry can give us the immense privilege of simply listening to people. It can also go beyond that. Ministering in an area where there had been many coal mines, but now they were closed, I had difficulty understanding the people. This was beyond my experience. I could listen to people, watch documentaries, use my imagination, but it was not the same as direct experience.

In another area, the community was predominantly rural. Farmers in the congregation had the rhythm of their lives dictated by the seasons and, it seemed, milking! The times of services allowed milking to be completed before in the morning or after in the afternoon. There I found out something of what that life was like. I'd worked on buses when I was younger and fishing trawlers, but I'd never milked a cow, so I asked a farmer in the congregation if I could join him. By breakfast on that morning I knew why he was a farmer and I was a minister! Nevertheless, a bond had developed in the process and my understanding had been deepened. Next time he spoke about his job, I had a better idea of what he was going on about.

'We used to have this chapel full on anniversaries.' You'll have heard this comment or will before long. Are there photos to provide evidence? Even if there are, what was it like the rest of the year? We can all wear rose-tinted spectacles sometimes. All the same, the reminiscences of older people can be invaluable in tapping into a real impression of the life and heritage of a congregation. Another benefit is that the time taken to listen to and value what you hear begins to build a relationship in a way that you and the storyteller may well cherish for a long time to come. Then, when you are in the full flow of a church meeting, what has been said will come back to you and you will realize that you are better informed, more effectively equipped to cope and have a greater understanding of the intransigence of a particular member of the meeting in relation to a specific issue than if you hadn't taken time to have those conversations. You will have started to uncover hidden agendas and allegiances that others may not know exist.

History is not just static. We should bring a critique to what we discover. It is important sometimes to challenge what we find. Ministry can have a prophetic edge that will enable change. Our task is not just to maintain what is but also ask why we are doing what we are doing. We should continually ask where we should be going from here to best serve God and our neighbours.

We have a responsibility to work lovingly with one another. That is the essence of the model of the body of Christ that Paul developed, at least in part, to counter the fragmented nature of the church in Corinth. To work with people requires understanding, not just of them as individuals but also the background and context that has caused them to be the way they are, react in the ways they do. The context is all-important.

What has been pictured here is the secular, cultural and sociological backdrop to ministry, but ministry in all its forms is founded on tradition, which is equally important.

The Church in England

The Protestant Church in England came out of the English Reformation and was, in the first instance, an Anglicized Church of Rome. Since then it has grown, diversified and has many different expressions. Methodists, Baptists, members of the United Reformed Church, Congregationalists, Unitarians, Pentecostalists, Free Evangelicals, Salvationists, Quakers, members of various black-led churches, Moravians and others, not to mention the Church of England, exist alongside one another.

The origins and traditions of these different groups have made them what they are and relations between them easy or difficult. Past experiences are formative and their effects can last from generation to generation. The Church of England values its Prayer Book, the history of which can be traced back to the genesis of the denomination before 1662. Members of the United Reformed Church value preaching and biblical scholarship, finding their roots in the Reformation. Most Baptist churches have a strong congregational ethos, stemming from times of alienation and persecution. Methodists have had a love-hate relationship with the Church of England, within which the denomination developed and then went on to create its own identity.

All of this is significant and the details can be traced in simple and more scholarly histories of each denomination. A working knowledge of our own denomination, a sense of our own identity, is important and may help us to understand better the people with whom we minister. It is not just in the past and irrelevant to today.

History is also important when we try to work ecumenically. We can better understand one another when we know the seat of our apparent prejudice.

Ministry in the light of history

We come by many different paths,
each certain that our way is true.
As sisters, brothers, let us talk,
a way to peace is overdue.

Caged in a creed, we think we've caught
the source of all that is to be,
but God cannot be thus confined:
the Spirit's flying, wild and free!

We think that we alone have found
the secret goal of all the earth;
we make our rules, oppress the weak,
with shackles hold them from their birth.

Within four walls we idolize
the treasures of our certainty.
We worship all that we have made.
Outside God sits in poverty.*

Within these histories of faith, it is worthwhile finding out where the people with whom we minister come from and what picture of the Church they give their allegiance to. It is also worth recognizing that we are part of an evolving living tradition – we make tradition as we go. Sometimes traditions have a very short history, but are still deeply ingrained. More often than not, the likelihood of moving someone from one position to another is slim. The purpose of this discernment, therefore, is to help us understand people better that we might care more effectively and better minister to one another's needs.

As this book unfolds it will explore patterns and areas of ministry with which some will feel comfortable and others will regard as anathema. At no point should we lose sight of the fact that those who hold opposing views – even if we are sure they are wrong from our perspective – are human and are God's children every bit as much as we are.

As we work alongside people of other denominations or none, we will work more effectively if we have some understanding of where they are coming from. This understanding should always be dynamic, open to learning and change. Often our impressions will be informed by prejudice. What other people think or believe is always more important than what we think they believe. This is a doubly important maxim when we seek to cross cultures or work with people of other faiths. Some may hope for a point to be reached where there is total mutual recognition and interchangeability of ministry between denominations. In the meantime, and perhaps more realistically, we should seek to work with respect, allowing for difference and not letting go of those things we value or our own integrity. It goes without saying that we should accord the same understanding to others that we would wish to be offered to ourselves.

* Andrew Pratt. Reproduced by permission of Stainer & Bell Ltd.

What about me?

There is a school of thought that suggests objectivity is impossible even within scientific research because, when we come to interpret data, we bring to it years of informed, or uninformed, prejudice. The same is true of ministry. So far I have concentrated on the importance of getting to know others and the contexts in which they are set. As we enter a new place, there are two directions that we can take. One is to say that, while we are new, we have the excuse, and the opportunity, to make changes. Sometimes this might be the right way forward, especially if we already have an understanding of the context where we are going and the confidence to carry through what we have in mind. All too soon, though, we will have adopted the culture of that place. Change will become more difficult.

The other alternative is to wait, observe, follow in the footsteps of our predecessor and do as she or he did. Only when we've had time to reflect, form an opinion and understand the context and the people will we begin to initiate change. Don't deceive yourself. If you take this second path, you will begin to change things from the moment you arrive, if not before. You are, or ought to be, your own person. That is not to say you are inconsiderate of others, their ways and customs, but, even if, for instance, you decide to adopt the same liturgy for communion as the previous minister, you will have your own intonation, manner and ways of doing things. We are never clones of one another. Your predecessor may have been a different gender, taller or shorter, more or less confident than you. For these reasons it is impossible to not change something, however hard you try.

What is immensely important is self-knowledge. Again and again in this book that will be underlined. Your culture, upbringing, theology, will all determine how you relate to others, how effectively you minister in different situations. The more self-aware you are, the less likely it is that you will hurt someone else unintentionally because of your own prejudice. It is possible to recognize those situations in which your own integrity and belief might be threatened or undermined, causing you to be defensive or unconstructive in your relationships with people.

> With daring we enter the future that beckons,
> our feelings in tension – excitement and fear.
> Wherever we're walking we know God walks with us,
> before and behind God's protection is near.
>
> So welcome the future and enter it boldly,
> look back, God was with you wherever you trod.
> This God is your lover through life and forever,
> take hold of the certainty: this is your God.

It is imperative to learn what your strengths and weaknesses are, what the limits of your comfort zone are in different situations. To give a single example, if you have been bereaved very recently, you might find it difficult ministering to someone in the same situation. You need that ministry yourself, so you might well use the pastoral relationship to meet your own needs rather than help the person for whom you are trying to care.

Summary

1. Know your context. Use every resource at your disposal to understand the situation in which you are ministering. This should include the long- and short-term history, geography, sociology, ethnography and politics of the area. Use books, people, the Internet and your own observations. Use them critically, questioning what you see and hear.
2. Know your people. Talk to them, listen to them, work with them. Take the time to do all of this and it will be repaid in terms of both the effectiveness of your ministry and the reduction in the stress you will experience as you minister.
3. Know yourself. Reflect on what your theology and background bring to the situation you are in. Try to understand those situations that are outside your experience and likely to bring you excitement or stress. Be aware that you are not alone in ministry. You do not have to minister in every situation. You do not have to provide the healing balm in every crisis.
4. You are part of the body of Christ and it has many members. Many of them can do what you're trying to do. Some may be able to do it better! Sometimes it's worth the risk of letting go, enabling someone else to minister, and recognizing that you don't know it all. You may be surprised at the results!

Looking ahead

*   How does your own upbringing and experience form the way you are, the things you like and what you do?
*   In what ways is your experience like that of those with whom you minister and in what ways is it different?
*   Can you really understand the people with whom you minister?
*   Does their culture and language make sense to you? Can you relate to it?
*   How can you get to understand them better?

Chapter 3
Leading worship

All together now: using all our gifts

I had just finished leading my first service in a new church. To my mind it had gone quite well – traditional, but with enough innovation to make me feel that I wasn't just regurgitating all they'd taught me in theological college. After all, that was a while ago and I was now an experienced minister.

I was greeted by a fresh-faced man in his twenties. 'I play guitar,' he said with a wry grin. Now how do you respond to that?

Looking back now, it was rather threatening. I might have had some experience, but this sounded as though I was going to be taken somewhere that I didn't want to go. 'Yes,' I responded and waited. He told me that, while he attended this church in the mornings, in the evenings he went to another church where he and his friends had a group – a couple played guitars, others keyboard and drums. They practised regularly and, I learned later, played proficiently.

Why had I responded like that? Well, he might have said 'I am part of a choir'. That might, at that stage, have been more to my taste – I had pretentions – but it would probably have made no difference. My position was that of the professional. I knew about liturgy, I was sure of the style and content of music that would support the worship I wanted to lead. Putting it another way, I was very insecure and needed to be in control of everything for my own safety. This young man unnerved me. As a result, I missed a, literally, God-sent, opportunity. His group never played in the church while I was ministering there.

Some time later in my ministry – when I had gained confidence, though I didn't know that was what had happened – I was met in a similar way by a member of a music group in a congregation where I was going to be the minister. On that occasion, we talked for a little while and then agreed a time when we could chat informally. We talked about likes and dislikes in music, the sorts of words that made a good song or a hymn, how best the skills of the music group could enhance what I felt I wanted to do, but also the ways in which their gifts could move and mould what I was doing in order to explore new avenues of worship. The breadth of material available for worship widened tremendously and everyone benefited. In addition, I was no longer the single 'load-bearer', which is a right perspective. Worship is the work of the whole people of God, not just entertainment provided by the person 'at the front'.

We live within the tension
of now and yet not yet,
we live in apprehension
but we will not forget
that God has been our guardian,
a lover and a friend,
and as we travel forward,
that presence will not end.

The seeds now sown among us
will flourish, thrive or die,
discoveries will charm us,
though some we will deny;
but God is never static,
our God will not stand still,
to follow after Jesus
will challenge, change and thrill.

So will you watch while waiting?
Or will you hear God's call
to climb the highest mountain?
Or will you fear to fall?
The risk that we are taking
is worth all we can give,
as moving on together
we learn how we can live.

In Paul's letters there is frequent reference to the Body of Christ as being a gathered community of people working together. It is a powerful image. If we believe that different people have different gifts and skills within the Church, then it makes sense to use those gifts and skills. The greatest stumbling block in the way of that process is the way in which the leader of a church works. How effectively you work will depend on your personality and experience, but some things can be learned. Working together is a principle that should be cherished and nurtured. Letting go of power and enabling others is a skill. Sometimes when we try to use it, it doesn't work. At other times it can be the means of releasing a congregation for worship and service.

It is worth reminding ourselves that, in many denominations, laypeople lead the majority of services. They are ministers in their own right. They have been trained and are sometimes better qualified than their ordained colleagues. They certainly have their feet on the ground and are often better able to relate the gospel to people who live their lives in a world that takes little if any account of the Church. That being the case, such preachers are equal colleagues, working as partners in God's work. We do that work a disservice if do not value all we can share with and receive from such a partnership. This process has its foundation in mutual respect, meeting and learning together and sharing in the planning of worship.

How do we go about working with others in worship?

The very first step involves self-knowledge. We need to ask ourselves what our calling is and what we do best.

If you are a gifted evangelist in the traditional sense, but have no musical skills, then your contributions to the music group are not likely to enhance worship or the life of the church, let alone your own reputation. It may even be that your gifts are best employed outside of an ordinary pastorate. Within a pastorate, you may need to use the skills of others to build up the congregation and engage in a teaching ministry to take people beyond the first call to discipleship.

The opposite is also true. If you do not have evangelistic skills, you may need to find those you can work beside who do have those skills. Perhaps you may find such skills among the qualified laypeople I have already mentioned.

These are simply examples to show that it is important we know those areas where we are best skilled and those where we are best supported by others. As ministry can sometimes be a lonely occupation, it is tempting to think that you are the only person who can do all the jobs. Very, very occasionally there may be a grain of truth in this but, more often than not, it is an excuse for either blocking others from being involved or being unwilling to take the time to enable others to discover and release their particular gifts.

Having recognized what we can do best ourselves, how can we work with others to lead worship?

It may be stating the obvious, but the obvious sometimes needs to be underlined. We need to talk with others, share with them, plan with them. To show you what I mean, let me take you through a number of scenarios, all of which are taken from actual experience.

Arriving at a church, I was told that, given a small amount of notice, it was possible to use any hymn in the hymnbook. It was a relatively new book that had been produced by the denomination three years before. When you hear this sort of thing, you take it with a pinch of salt. To begin with I played safe, choosing only those hymns the congregation was bound to know.

How can we be sure what they will know, though? I had a reminder just a few weeks ago of how careful we must be. Going to another church, one that I had not been to before, I chose four hymns thoroughly well known throughout my denomination – or so I thought. In that church two out of the four had never been sung before!

So, to return to the above example, I also didn't rely just on what I thought they could sing or on what the choir leader said they could sing. I sat down with the choir leader and asked when they had sung particular hymns that I wanted to use. We discussed those items that were new and decided together when to introduce them and how. Choices as to whether a single voice or an instrument would give the best introduction to a melody line were left to the choir leader. There was much discussion, though, as time went on and we built a relationship of trust. It made things easier to rely on each other and know things would work in our own particular areas of expertise.

Another time, the organist of a small church rang up to ask for the hymn numbers a week in advance of a service. He only played occasionally and I soon discovered that this was his practice. I can't play the organ at all and I am glad of any help I can get with music, but, on one occasion, he used the same tune twice in one service, for two different hymns. The congregation gave me a quizzical look as we entered into the second hymn – those who noticed! Of course they wondered what I was playing at, but he'd chosen the tunes.

Later that week, I had occasion to call on him again. It was coming up to Easter. I thought I'd talk with him about the hymns for the weekend and also enquire, sensitively, about his choice of tune. We sat in his bungalow drinking tea. Then I brought out the hymns for the weekend. I was biding my time, looking for the right moment to raise the question of the repeated tune. As he looked over the hymns for the week ahead, his eye lighted on 'When I survey the wondrous cross'. For those who know about these things, the tune was Rockingham – one most commonly set to these words. 'Oh, you can't have that,' said my friend. 'Why on earth not?' I asked. He looked at me for a moment. 'It goes too high!' I remonstrated with him. It was my father's favourite and, anyway, it had been sung for years, and to that tune, and it had never been too high before. My temper was fraying. What did he mean?

'It's the way I play it,' was the reply. Very sheepishly he confessed that his musical ability in the traditional sense was very limited. He played 'by ear'. He only knew a few tunes – those he had already heard. It was true, he could play to entertain and people enjoyed listening to him, but there were limits. He only played in one key and, he was right, the way he played 'When I survey the wondrous cross' was unsingable! My feelings softened. I no longer felt angry. His vulnerable admission had built a bond. From that day on, we chose the hymns together whenever he was playing. Some of the power had been transferred and everybody benefited.

'John would like to read in chapel,' said his mum. That was not a plea for me to allow this, but, rather, to warn me. John was 30 and had learning difficulties. He couldn't read, but he did have a strong clear voice and an even stronger faith. She knew that he was going to ask me if he could read at a service. After all, others went and stood behind the lectern and did that.

Now, I'm a pacifist, but a pre-emptive strike seemed in order. The next time I met John, I asked him if he would like to read. He was thrilled to bits. I got out a Bible and asked if he could make it out. I know other people with disabilities who read very well but have been discouraged and made to feel that they shouldn't or couldn't, but John really could not read. 'OK,' I said, 'here's the plan.'

The following Sunday, I announced that John was going to read the gospel. By this time I'd confided in his mother so she didn't have apoplexy! As he came forward, there was a sharp intake of breath from the congregation. The looks on their faces expressed a mix of horror and concern. John and I stood together by the lectern. I whispered the words of the gospel reading and he repeated them in a clear, loud voice. When he walked back to his seat, he did so with his head held high and his mother half beaming and half moved to tears. The effect on the congregation was far more wide-reaching and profound than usually accompanies, or follows, the reading.

Sometimes it is easy to believe in God. I was having difficulty finding people to fill pulpit appointments, particularly in the evenings. Preachers then often had small congregations. Simultaneously, a member of the church said that she had an idea for a service and could we follow it up sometime. I met with her and talked this through. She had drawn together so much material that there would be little room for anything that I might want to add. In any case, what she had was coherent and complete in itself. An idea began to form in my mind and we talked it through.

People in churches can get very uptight if the 'wrong person' is leading worship. Even in freer charismatic churches this can be so. So, we struck on the idea of me introducing the service – both a week before in our notices and on the evening in question – so that it was given appropriate support, the minister 'was there'. I could also absorb any flack.

The service took place. Joan had gathered around her people from the congregation with different gifts and skills. There was music, prayer, Bible readings, reflection, singing. Because the congregation respected her and owned what was happening, there were at least twice the normal number of people present. Everyone agreed, it was a beautiful act of worship.

Now here's the rub. I have to admit that the rules of my denomination don't allow for someone who is not trained and recognized in some way to lead worship. Oh dear! I'd got round this because I believed that Joan had the gifts and graces to lead this one act of worship. I covered myself by preparing the ground, informing colleagues of what was happening and being there on the day and taking responsibility for the service, even though I had had little part in preparing or leading it.

What followed was wonderful. Others asked if they could do the same and some were asked if they would. As a consequence, over a period of time, that congregation began to develop their own skills in leading worship. My role was to provide as much or as little support as those leading the worship needed. Sometimes individuals were involved, sometimes friends, on occasion a whole family. I asked to see an order of service and only to be involved in the leading if they wanted me to be. Whenever possible, I was in the congregation. Over a period of time, worship ranged from times of meditation to choruses and small choir items, through to dance and drama. Without exception, the attendance rates for these acts of worship were greater than for other times.

> Dare we take risks
> > carefully?

The next step is to 'export' these acts of worship to other churches or, better still, encourage other congregations to explore their gifts and skills that they might be shared for the benefit of all.

To preach or not to preach

Preaching pre-dates Christianity. Proclaiming and interpreting the word of God to people and for people has always been necessary. Prophets were preachers. Jesus began his ministry with a sermon and so did Peter on the day of Pentecost. That having been said, preaching isn't always an easy option.

'What about original sin?' were the words he greeted me with at the door – no hand outstretched, just a piercing look in his eye. He had been listening. I had missed something. That was many years ago.

Years later at an ecumenical event in a large church, keeping faith with my own integrity, I preached from the heart. Halfway through the sermon, a man got up, walked noisily to the back of the church, slammed down his hymnbook and walked out. He'd been listening, too. I wish he'd stayed to the end!

The gospel can be offensive, it can be scandalous. Sometimes it will move people – literally! It still needs to be proclaimed, but how?

Is there any point in preaching?

'The age of the sermon is dead . . . long live the sermon!'

I believe that there is a point to preaching, but also that there is good reason for 'preaching' being used as a pejorative term. Historically, preachers have used argument and persuasion in equal amounts to communicate truths. Today, the very idea of truth may be contested.

Often the illustrations used were taken from sources that were remote from the people hearing them. As a result, identification with the message being preached was difficult or impossible. Even when the illustration being used was contemporary it was often either obscure or quoted out of context. If we quote from a television programme, for instance, we are depending on people having seen it. Not everyone watches the same things or reads the same newspapers. The most vivid quotation or allusion is wasted on us if we don't understand it.

For some, it is imperative that the sermon be based on the Bible. Frequently this can mean that the preacher regurgitates the content of the latest (sometimes not the latest!) commentary. You might find that Bible notes you are using yourself are repeated back to you. At worst, we are taken on a tour of exposition that seeks to dissect a passage in minute detail, giving each nuance of the Greek or Hebrew text. At the opposite end of the scale, a preacher, making the excuse of having been 'busy', tells us things that we can read straight out of the Bible, adding nothing that grasps our attention. If there is an illustration, it has not been thought through.

It is dangerous to take topical issues and comment on them from the pulpit. You may have an expert in your congregation. There may even be, heaven forbid, a theologian hidden there! In one of my congregations, there was an elderly farmer and his wife. When I visited them pastorally, I discovered that they had only recently moved to the area and he was a very competent and well-informed organist, though he was losing his sight, and she had a degree in theology from Oxford University. We had some interesting conversations!

Visiting an elderly people's home to lead worship, I was going round after the brief act of worship talking with the people. Coming up to a man, I shook his hand. He muttered something incomprehensible. Feigning that I had not heard him, my assumption was that he was senile and speaking gibberish, I asked him to repeat what he had said. As I listened, something in the words he was saying began to ring bells. He was repeating back to me the verses on which I'd spoken, the opening of the Gospel according to John, but he was saying it in Greek! He was certainly not senile – he had remembered the Greek from his schooldays. Never underestimate the intellect or understanding of the people you are speaking to – a lesson I had to learn.

With all these pitfalls is preaching still worthwhile?

I believe it is, but it ought to come with a health warning – 'preaching can seriously damage a congregation's spiritual health'! If we are going to use this opportunity effectively, we need to know what it is we are trying to do. Then we need to look at what we are doing to see if it really can achieve our purpose – not just with an ideal group of people, but with the real people in our church.

Traditionally, preaching has been seen as didactic – which means teaching – and kerygmatic – exhorting or encouraging. For either, we have to have people's attention. We need to use language that they understand. We need to be simple, but not simplistic. It is easy to be patronizing or offer glib solutions to problems that have taxed theologians for millennia.

We need, as far as we are able, to know the people with whom we are sharing worship. That involves solid pastoral work and intelligent listening. If you don't think that's worthwhile, what does it say about how you value people? Think just how much money is spent by organizations on consumer research in order to get people to buy products or to make services relevant to them. This is your equivalent of consumer research, but it may have far more significant consequences.

I heard an agricultural chaplain talking about the amount of time he spent listening to farmers who were trying to come to terms with the effects of foot and mouth disease in cattle. As a result, when he preached, he spoke their language. He understood their fears. He had watched them try to keep a business afloat. His sermons were not 'All things bright and beautiful' or even 'Jesus is Lord, creation's voice proclaims it'. For his hearers, those words would simply not ring true.

The minister returning from the bedside of a young woman who had had a miscarriage preached differently at a baptism on Sunday. She knew that conception and birth could bring fear and anguish as well as joy and celebration.

Entering a new year, the vicar of a village that had been decimated by an air crash was aware the year past had brought little celebration, little in the way of experience to firm up faith for his congregation. A lament from a Psalm informed the New Year sermon, giving people permission to cry in anguish, to pour out doubt.

So, the people need to know, when you stand there, that you know them, understand them; that you weep with them and laugh with them. Only you will have the privilege of intimate knowledge about so many of the people there waiting for your words. Choose them carefully, speak with gentleness, preach with understanding.

If you're going to preach . . .
for God's sake do it well!

Be honest in your preaching. Say what you believe, even if that might sometimes be unexpected. (It was only when I took the risk of admitting that I found some parts of Scripture as hard to take as the members of my congregation that my preaching on these passages had integrity.) Then the congregation will listen because they need to hear what you have to say. Like all good news, it will make them feel better and be better people. On the way, we who minister may become better people ourselves – with a double helping of grace and a dusting of humility.

So, if we're going to preach, how do we go about it?

Many years ago I went to a religious convention. It was a large gathering with a preacher speaking each evening for a week. He talked for about an hour and had everyone's rapt attention. That runs counter to all I've said. It shouldn't have worked. I bought some recordings of the sessions. A few months later, I was pottering about the house and thought I'd listen to them while I was doing one or two other things. I was in the other room when I heard the preacher's voice. I've no idea what he was saying, but the way he spoke – simply the tone of his voice and his use of language – commanded my attention. I either had to listen or turn off the recording.

Next time you preach, make a recording of yourself. Listen to it, critically. If what you're saying doesn't catch your attention or make you want to listen, it's unlikely to engage a congregation. After all, you were moved enough by all of this to want to share it, so what you are trying to say is of vital importance. If that's not true then why did you say it? This is harsh, but I have to ask: are you in the right vocation?

Of course, it could be that you are really convinced of the importance of what you are saying, but it's just not coming over. If that's so, then it could be due to a number of things. Your tone of voice or the manner of your delivery may be at fault. Some voice coaching might help. You could also listen to other communicators and, without mimicking them, try to learn why they hold people's attention and you don't.

If all this feels like too much effort, not worth it, I have to ask you that hard question again.

If the sound of your voice is all right, then what about the content of what you're saying? If you have something to communicate, be it teaching or encouragement, it's worth preparing well. Rehearsing how you deliver a sermon can help (providing you don't rehearse so much that you get bored with what you're saying by the time you preach), but the content is important, too.

Let's assume that you are beginning with a Bible passage. Read it through. When you have finished, without looking up a commentary, quickly write down the single words that come into your mind. Don't think, just play a word association game with yourself. Use the words to make a sentence or two. You may well have got to the nub of what you need to say.

If the passage has no effect on you at all, then perhaps another might work. The lectionary can help, but following it slavishly can prevent you from communicating as well as you might. Gradually build up a story. That's the key to the effectiveness of that convention preacher, too. It wasn't just the delivery of the words, he was a storyteller and you need to be too.

Here's another way into producing a sermon. Take the Bible story and imagine yourself as one of the characters. What do you see? What do you hear? How do you feel? Write down descriptions using the sort of language that you would use in conversation every day – avoid theological language. Then, when you preach, you can begin to draw your listeners into the story. Ask them, rhetorically or directly, how they would feel, what they would see if they were there. In this way, the stories begin to come alive, the characters feel real. In addition, we begin to understand why people respond in the way they do because we're human and we'd behave like that, too. Suddenly, we realize that the reason behind these stories having been kept through the ages is that they are about real people, encountering real issues and these issues are timeless. As we become more skilled, we can draw relevant parables out of present experience.

Every time we preach, it is as though we are telling something precious, something special. It is as though we are having a conversation with an individual. When we have a conversation, it is never one-sided – if it is, that's a monologue. We may, on occasion, get or elicit a response from a congregation. If we do, then it is important that we demonstrate we have heard it and respond appropriately. I remember once talking to a primary school class that I was trying to teach. A little girl responded, 'I've got pink shoes.' What she was saying was irrelevant to the discussion, but, until I'd engaged with her about them, I wasn't going to get any further. If you ask a question, you need to deal with the response you get and not the one you wish you'd got.

> Worship that absorbs our being:
> God transcendent, in this place!
> Glancing, shifting, dancing spirit,
> immanent, the source of grace.
>
> Struggle, mild or monumental,
> faith unfound or blazing clear,
> singing, sustenance and weeping,
> carves God's presence, mystic, near.
>
> Face to face with God we honour
> values that the Christ would crown,
> when we risk divine communion,
> see the world turned upside down.

More often than not, you won't ask for or get a verbal response, but you will get a response neverthless. A yawn or a laugh communicate things you need to hear. A nod or a shake of the head can hint at something you need to underline and affirm or say again in a different way. To know what is happening, you need eye contact. To respond, you cannot be tied to a script. There is more to this preaching business than meets the eye and it is no wonder that much preaching is not as good as it could be.

The ideal is to know the story you are going to tell so well that you need no notes or, at most, pointers. If you are telling a friend about a holiday that you enjoyed, you don't write it out first and your enthusiasm shines through. It's not that you're unprepared, but you are so well prepared that if someone, by a look in their eyes, says, 'What does that mean?' you can respond by saying something like, 'Of course this is not as straightforward as it seems. Let's look at it another way . . .' Wait for the nod and then go on, otherwise at least one member of your congregation is no longer with you.

It is a good rule of thumb to begin your preparation a week ahead. That gives you time to think, to digest your material, look at it in different ways, write it out if you need to and internalize it. Only when you have a pretty good idea of where you are going should you check anything you need to with a commentary. Why have I left this till last? Simply because you are theologically trained. You know all the technicalities. Most of your congregation will not. Preparing in this way, making immediate responses to the gospel, puts you in their situation. You are now more likely to communicate effectively with them. The only purpose of the commentary is to make sure that anything you say about the story, the way you are interpreting it, is valid.

Similarly, if you comment on a news item, check your facts and be as well informed as you can, even if you don't use all the information at your disposal.

Do we have to preach?

We do need to communicate the gospel, but preaching, in the traditional sense, is not the only way to do it. This is not a resource book so we can just touch the surface here with a few ideas to get you started. Nothing is new and nothing here claims to be.

To begin, picture two people in a church, each standing behind a lectern on either side.

Reader 1: Psalm 22.

Reader 2: Psalm 121.

Reader 1: Excuse me! I thought you asked me to read Psalm 22?

Reader 2: I did, but I thought you weren't going to start, so I thought I should.

Reader 1: But you're not reading the same psalm.

Reader 2: No. I'm reading Psalm 121.

Reader 1: So you don't want me to read Psalm 22?

Reader 2: Yes I do and I also want to read number 121.

Reader 1: Two psalms? Are you sure?

Reader 2: Absolutely!

Reader 1: Sounds strange to me. Anyway, who goes first? I suppose it should be you, seeing as you're the visitor.

Reader 2: Oh, no! Surely it should be ladies first?

Reader 1: Maybe, but in the opinion of some of those people out there, I'm no lady!

Reader 2: We're wasting time! How are we going to resolve this?

Reader 1: I know! Let's be different. Let's read alternate verses. You start!

Reader 2: Psalm 121.

Reader 1: Psalm 22.

Reader 2: 'I lift up my eyes to the hills – where has my help come from?'

Reader 1: 'My God, my God, why have you forsaken me? Why are you so far from saving me, from the words of my groaning?'

Reader 2: 'My help comes from the Lord, the maker of heaven and earth.'

Reader 1: 'O my God, I cry out by day, but you do not answer, by night and am not silent.'

Reader 2: 'He will not let your foot slip – he who watches over you will not slumber.'

Reader 1: Excuse me a minute!

Reader 2: Yes! What now?

Reader 1:   Are we reading from the same book?

Reader 2:   I hope so! Mine's a Bible and you're reading from the church Bible.

Reader 1:   Well, I think there's some kind of discrepancy.

Reader 2:   Do you indeed? What is it now?

Reader 1:   Well, whoever wrote my psalm couldn't seem to find God anywhere. Your man knows exactly where to find him. So my man goes round shouting, 'Where are you, God? I want to talk to you!' while yours just ambles off to the hillside to find him.

Reader 2:   Yes! Well, they were probably two very different people.

Reader 1:   But which of them do I believe? All these contradictions! I give up! I'm going – and I'll just let you get on with trying to explain that one!

Reader 2:   I can't get my head around that!

Marjorie Dobson

So we begin and what comes next?

- Open discussion among the congregation.
- Offer a reflection on the contradiction between the two psalms and the way this mirrors contradiction in other parts of the Bible.

There are a number of ways in which a dialogue of this sort can be used. The advantage is that all is required is two competent readers. There is no script to be learned.

This is a simple way into the dramatic representation of Scripture. Monologues imagining the situations of different characters can also bring the gospel to life. Someone in your congregation may be able to produce something of this sort to order. Alternatively, there are collections produced by organizations such as the Iona Community (see under Bell in the Resources section for this chapter) or authors such as Marjorie Dobson or Paul Glass that can be pressed into service. It is important not to use the same style every time or it can become a cliché.

Dance or music on their own can also interpret or represent ideas, feelings, emotions, stories.

There is a vast array of ideas available for all ages, ranging from Fresh Expressions and Godly Play to puppets, musicals and oratorio.

In all of these, it is critical – as it is with all preaching – to be sure of what is being communicated so that the message does not get lost in the medium used to communicate it.

Summary

1. Ask not 'what can I do for a congregation?' but, rather, 'what can we do together?'
2. In the context of worship, answer the following questions.
    -   What are your own gifts and skills and what are your limits?
    -   How can you enable others to use their gifts?
    -   How can you give others confidence in the use of their gifts and skills?
    -   Ask yourself, what is the best way to communicate in this context with these people?
3. When preaching:
    -   never underestimate your hearers
    -   know your congregation
    -   tell stories
    -   listen to and watch your congregation while you preach
    -   think of preaching as conversation.

Looking ahead

-   Get to know your congregation.
-   Work with others.
-   Enable others.
-   Explore different methods of communication.

Chapter 4
First contacts – basic principles

Tread gently for you are treading on my faith

I was walking past a department store in the town where I live. Someone I've known for a few years called out to me. I crossed over and we chatted. He was moving house soon. Quite out of the blue he said, 'I'm not sure if I was ever christened. When all this is sorted out, would you help me to find out and, if I wasn't, do it for me?'

Here was a man nearing retirement for whom baptism, though he didn't use the word, was of immense significance, significant enough to ask a minister about even though he's no regular churchgoer, even though this was something that he felt should have happened when he was a child. That sort of request can put you on your back foot. I'm reminded of the story of Philip and the Ethiopian eunuch.

> As they were going along the road, they came to some water and the eunuch said, 'Look, here is water! What is to prevent me from being baptized?'

> (Acts 8.36)

How do we respond to requests like that? It's significant that, for Philip, the answer was given in an action – no preparation, no question, no creedal confession, just this:

> He commanded the chariot to stop, and both of them, Philip and the eunuch, went down into the water, and Philip baptized him.

> (Acts 8.38)

Of course there was follow-up! Well, read the passage for yourself:

> When they came up out of the water, the Spirit of the Lord snatched Philip away; the eunuch saw him no more, and went on his way rejoicing.

> (Acts 8.39)

If I can misquote a poem for a moment, tread gently for you are treading on another person's faith. That faith may be frail, it may be flawed, the person talking to you may be using the 'wrong' language, he or she may not understand what he or she is asking for, but, in situations like these, we are confronted by human beings like us.

I remember, as a child, being in a maths lesson at school. The teacher asked what a congruent triangle was. I, foolishly, put up my hand. 'One that fits slap bang on top of another one' was my response. There was sharp intake of breath from the class. He and they were expecting something to do with angles and lengths of sides. The teacher paused just long enough to think. 'That's exactly right, but more often we'd put it like . . .' He went on to explain the proper mathematical terms. I can't remember them. I can't remember the teacher's name. I can remember, though, that moment of grace when I risked being a fool and was affirmed when I could feel my contemporaries were waiting for me to be put down. Perhaps there's a rule for ministry there.

Imagine that something immensely significant has happened to you. What do you do? Well, I suppose it depends what it is. If you've won the Lottery, you might want to keep it secret! Otherwise, if the news is good, it's not long before you're on the phone, firing off an e-mail or writing a letter. We all have an intrinsic need to share those things that are good and celebrate them. Such celebrations make more sense in company. Dancing round your room on your own may be a start, but you'll soon run out of steam. On the other hand, if the news is bad, you choose carefully how you handle it, but most people, sooner or later, choose someone with whom to share it. A burden shared is a burden halved, as the saying goes, and there's some truth in it.

None of this is religious in the formal sense, but it seems to have a deep root in our humanity.

It is interesting to me that those societies which have sought to be consciously atheist, where religion has been banned, seek, nevertheless, to mark valued occasions, whether individual or corporate. I can remember, in the days of the USSR, that May Day celebrations in the Red Square in Moscow were carried out with military precision, but also with an almost religious attention to detail. Equally, members of the National Secular Society seek to mark birth and death in ways that are not religious, without reference to God, but with a profound sense of the importance of the person and what is happening. Again, people marry or enter into civil partnerships without religious ceremonies, but with a sense of solemnity that would not be out of place for a religious gathering and often using a pattern (I hesitate to use the word 'liturgy') of words that those who are both religious and observant will notice parallel liturgies used in churches. In this context, it interested me a few years ago when I was enlisted to help a local registrar of marriages put together a suitable secular ceremony that could be used at the registry office or in other secular settings.

Less formally, we celebrate significant birthdays – eighteenths, twenty-firsts, sixtieths, sixty-fifths, seventieths, eightieths and so on – with parties and gifts that are more significant than those for the intervening birthdays. None of this requires religion and any suggestion that they are religious would be frowned on by many.

I have gone to some length to indicate these times of celebration, these markers of significant occasions, because I sense that they pre-date religious observance and are deeply rooted in our individual or corporate psyches. That observation may enable us to understand better the way in which people who have no religious affiliation often seek the ministrations of the Church at times that are important to them. It may also explain why they are surprised, or perhaps even offended, when members of the Church they have asked look at them askance, wondering why they are seeking its offices. From their perspective this is what the Church does, in much the same way that a garage services cars or a supermarket sells food. If my presupposition is correct, then we must be very careful how we handle these approaches, particularly if we see them as opportunities for mission.

> What is this blasphemy we hear?
> That God is here? We see God's face?
> We look around, we look again,
> yes, God is here within this place.
>
> What is this beauty all around?
> God's 'face' in everyone we see?
> Each neighbour, enemy or friend,
> God's spirit in each one and me.
>
> Anointed, chosen, called by God,
> we talk the words that Jesus talked.
> We do the things that Jesus did,
> we walk the path that Jesus walked.

So, someone wants to get married or have their child baptized or they are bereaved. How do we respond? Are there any ground rules? For me, there are two critical elements that come before everything else. Let us look at these.

What does the Church expect of me as its representative?

Your congregation or your denomination may well have regulations that they will rightly assume apply to you. Sometimes these will be set down quite clearly, as a rubric in a service book or as a set of standing orders or expectations. For some, they will be encapsulated in Canon Law. Overlaying, or under-girding, all of this, depending how you see it, will be the law of the land. All of these are significant and of varying degrees of importance. What is imperative is your knowledge of these factors and how they both constrain and enable your ministry.

Ordinarily, you won't be expected to negotiate with the law of the land. It is in statute and it is your obligation to abide by it. That said, a proper prophetic ministry will challenge those laws and statutes that are wrong. The law of your denomination may be equally binding (and equally open to challenge). If the expectation is that infants are baptized in appropriate circumstances, then you need to have a willingness to work within this framework. Similarly, if it is accepted that anyone living within the parish boundaries has a right to the services of the Church, you need to know how you can work effectively with this. Congregational expectations can sometimes be just as strict and, again, we must be ready to challenge these when we have to. For Baptist congregations, conditions for membership may be enshrined in the deeds and covenants that established the particular congregation and they will be as binding as a covenant concerning the use of land or property. They are not negotiable.

Within these constraints, individual congregations may well have their own expectations. These are not enshrined in law, but they need to be known and recognized. There is often a sense of 'we always do it this way' and it may not be transparently clear what 'this way' is, so it is best to ask. Then, if you are going to offend anyone, at least you know that you are going to do it and you can prepare for the consequences. Generally, it is good counsel to avoid causing offence, to go with the flow, even if it isn't exactly what you would wish to do. The people of the church were probably there before you came and will most likely outlast you. They know the place and its people.

This brings us to the other element.

What do we expect of ourselves?

I can't answer this question for you, but it is important that you answer it for yourself. It may be that, in the course of ministry, you'll need to answer it more than once. Let me frame the sorts of questions that will need to be faced. In later chapters I'll look at some examples of scenarios that have really happened. Then we can firm up your answers, but, to begin with, let's start with broad generalities. If you know the answers, skip the questions!

How do you see the Church? Whose Church is it anyway?

If your understanding of the Church is that it is a closed order, then that has particular consequences.

Most people confronted by this sort of question respond by saying, 'Oh, the Church is for everyone', but what is the reality? Are you happy with everyone coming to the church where you minister in whatever state, whatever their attitude to you and everyone else there? How does your body language work when you are confronted by someone who is radically different in behaviour, dress or language to yourself and those around you?

You see your church, and you as minister, may not be as open as you think.

Then again, what expectations are placed on people who wish to receive Communion? Are the conditions different if it is a child? What about someone of another denomination? I remember a prominent Roman Catholic Monsignor once talking to a group of ordinands and seminarians about Communion. He was set a question to trick him. The conversation went a bit like this:

'Whose table do you preside at at the Mass?'
'The Lord's Table.'
'So doesn't your church say that only confirmed Catholics can come
    to the Table?'
'That's right.'
'But it's the Lord's Table.'
'Yes' – and this was what the questioner was after – 'everyone is
    welcome here.'
You could almost hear the cry of 'Gotcha!'
'So what if one of us Protestants joins the line to come to you
    tomorrow morning at Mass wanting the bread.'

There was ever such a slight pause and, with a look of gentle, understanding kindness, the Monsignor responded, 'I will give you the bread . . . but please don't do that to me.'

The conditions for receipt of Communion in this instance were quite clear, but this man knew exactly where he stood and he also knew the expectations of the Church, of which he was a representative. In a similar situation, how would we respond?

Are we able to be true to our denomination or congregation and put limits on how we receive people and respond to them? Does our interpretation of the Bible in relation to, say, divorce or homosexuality, lead us to want to impose or express certain expectations or conditions on people. If that is so, how, then, do we ensure we still treat others as valued children of God or don't they fit this category?

It becomes clear that our day-to-day actions as ministers – lay or ordained – are informed by our ecclesiology, theology, way of interpreting Scripture, culture, prejudice . . .. Need I go on? As we are dealing day to day with real people who matter to God, it is crucial that we get it right.

A student amazed and humbled me the other day. 'I remember what you said in one of those introductory sessions two years ago – it stayed with me.' Then she repeated word for word what I had forgotten I'd said – something that had been a throwaway remark, off the cuff.

Be careful what you say . . .
                    it may be used in evidence against you!

Many years ago, my mother was set against the Church by an insignificant but ill-thought action. This is history again, so bear with me! It was before the days when antibiotics became regularly available. My dad, I'm told, had pneumonia. He'd been off work and hadn't been to the church that he attended for months. He had been actively involved there when he was fit. After about six months, someone came. His opening words were, 'We haven't had Ted's envelopes' (shorthand for collection). From that day forward, my mother had little time for the Church – 'They're hypocrites, only after your money,' she'd say.

Much later, the intrinsic 'rite of passage' gene kicked in, though. I was coming up to the age of 16 and she felt that the Church ought to mark it! Strange, given her views. She had been a Methodist. Dad still was – he'd not been put off. I was somewhere between atheism and superstition. Mum went to the local Anglican vicar and suggested that it would be good if both I and my dad were confirmed. Sounds like Mum was a little crazy. She wasn't – she was behaving like someone who was searching quite desperately for a church that believed in her, as God believed in her, in spite of the fact that the servant of the Church of her birth seemed to have denied that value.

Perhaps we've come full circle to where we came in – my friend wanting to be 'christened', not knowing if he had been or not. I wonder why he got missed out? Was it because his family were Baptists or was it something to do with his parents or the prejudice of the Church? Who knows? I won't until I ask. That question may be hurtful or insensitive. You see, until you ask, you don't know where people are coming from. 'Philip and the eunuch, went down into the water, and Philip baptized him.' Is that the way, perhaps? No questions asked. Affirm my friend and leave the rest to God? Can I do that? Will my Church let me? Should I do that?

What are your preconceived ideas about these people who just 'use the Church'? Is that all they're doing? Is your attitude more a form of defence or a need to have some control? It may not be, but you need to know not only what you are doing but, as far as you can, the motive you have for what you are doing.

I come back to the question, whose Church is it? Here are some more.

Who are you? What is your role? To whom are you accountable? What does ordination 'do'?

Well, at one level, you are no different from anyone else. You are a valued child of God and God loves you. The likelihood is that you undervalue yourself. For clergy, it is often a hazard, but one that is rooted deep in slightly suspect Christian theology. Talking about food, God is reported to have said to Peter, 'What God has made clean, you must not call profane.' You are of value because God made you. How dare you say otherwise? Yet, we have it drummed into us, 'it is not I but Christ within me', 'I am but a worm' and so on. Those passages of Scripture that are supposed to generate a right sense of humility so often produce in us a poor self-image and low self-worth. That is almost blasphemous! Remember again, you are a valued child of God.

Read all the papers and reports that your denomination provides to help you to understand what your role is and to whom you are accountable.

For some, it is clear that, at ordination or whatever Church process separates us for ministry, an irrevocable change takes place as a consequence of the action of the Holy Spirit. Technically, the change is ontological. Our very being is different from that point on. If that is the understanding of your Church or your own personal view of ordination, then the consequences are far-reaching, helpful, yet onerous.

I have been ordained as a minister of Word and Sacrament of my denomination. From an ontological perspective, that simple, yet profound, act of ordination means that, regardless of my own feelings or opinion, from that day forward I am different. Others may recognize it in formal or functional ways, but whether they do or not doesn't matter. From that moment on I have been different. There is a great reassurance in this as the initiative is with God. However I may feel, however others may treat me, God has made me different. This is a divine risk of grace. My ministry is God's responsibility, not my own, and no one can undo that. Once a priest, always a priest.

The flipside of that is it places an immense responsibility on the person who has an ontological view of ordination. There is a need to grow into the grace that we believe has been conferred by the laying on of hands for, surely we are not yet as Christ would have us be. The concept is audacious.

For others, ministry is a matter of role or function. Technically, again, this is teleological. Someone with this point of view believes that they have been set apart for a particular purpose, for a role. The role may be time-limited and may change. They do a particular task. The Church, under the guidance of God's Spirit, has decided that they have the gifts and graces to do the job. This feels as though there is a far closer human link to what is going on. It should generate a corporate sense of responsibility. This is not just God working, but the Church working with God. There is also an understanding that a particular role may change or even come to an end.

The flipside of this view is that it feels less onerous, but it can also feel more insecure. If the role ends or changes, the sense of vocation can feel threatened. If I am no different, intrinsically, from anyone else, what has ordination 'done'?

One of these perspectives may be more attractive to you than the other. Which you favour may depend on your theological position, background and experience and observations of other people in the same role. What is interesting is that, if you find yourself at one extreme or the other, you will discover as your ministry progresses that it is tinged with aspects of the other extreme. If you favour the ontological/being understanding, you will frequently find your role being defined by what you do. If you lean towards the teleological/functional interpretation, from time to time other people will treat you as though you are different because they perceive you as being different.

In terms of your day-to-day ministry, how you respond to different circumstances and people will, to some extent, depend on your theology of ordination. If you know that you are being influenced in this way, then you have a means of monitoring your ministry. It will enable you to understand to whom you are accountable and whether that accountability relates to your denominational expectations or something that is more particularly rooted in your own understanding. To say that we are not accountable to our denomination denies our allegiance to that institution and, if this is what we think, we should be 'considering our position'. To say that you are simply accountable to God is a cop-out. In ministry, we are accountable to the elderly person needing a visit, the young unmarried mother, the crying child as they each represent Christ to us and we Christ to them. We are also accountable to our colleagues, whether in a structural sense, in terms of line management, or, less formally, as sisters and brothers under God.

First and foremost, those who approach us as ministers of the Church are coming in need and deserve God's grace or at least our kindness, even if they could not put this expectation into words and even if it does not fit our understanding of them.

Summary

1. Ask yourself these questions.
    *   Did I make this decision or treat this person in this way because that is best for them?
    *   Will my attitude to them build them up in God's love and in faith?
    *   Is my theological prejudice likely to diminish anyone else as a human being?
    *   Will they go away from me better than when they came?
    *   Have I affirmed them?

2. Remember: prejudice can often masquerade as theology.

Looking ahead

*   What is your view of ordination?
*   What is your view of the Church?
*   To whom are you personally accountable?
*   What is your view of those from outside the Church coming to church for occasional services (baptisms or weddings)?

Chapter 5
Baptism – children or adults?

Baptizing a dog

The phone rang and I picked it up. 'Could you baptize my dog please?' Honestly, that's what the woman on the other end said! How did I respond? No 'yes' or 'no'. 'Can I come round and talk with you?' She said I could, there and then. I suggested she put the kettle on.

Over a cup of tea, she told me her story. Her mother had died and her only company during the day was her dog. Her husband worked nights. The dog was a puppy and could be quite noisy. Her husband had said that if it didn't quieten down she'd have to get rid of it. So 'logically' she asked me to baptize it, 'so it would behave itself'!

I tell this story for a number of reasons. To begin with, it's true. It demonstrates the way in which the first things that people come to ministers with are not always the ones that are really bothering them – counsellors call this a 'presenting problem'. We need to listen and learn when we are confronted by an unusual request, not just dismiss it out of hand. This story could equally well have begun a chapter on bereavement.

The story also demonstrates the shallow understanding that some people have of the sacraments, but also the hope that they invest in the Church and its representatives, its ministers. In addition, this specific request presses us to think again about baptism and what it means. I had to offer this woman, who had made a request in innocence and hope, an answer that did not belittle her but affirmed her and gave her realistic hope and still matched what I knew to be true of the sacraments of the Church. If I had just said, 'We don't baptize dogs', I would have been selling her short and missed an opportunity to allow God to offer grace and hope, love and reassurance.

Let me tell you a little more. I asked why she wanted the dog baptized and what she thought my doing that would achieve. I then explained that baptism is a way in which people are incorporated into the Church and that adults say something of their faith and belief within the service. I spoke of the promises that the parents of infants might say. I then asked her if she thought this made sense in relation to her dog. She was no fool and could see that it didn't. 'What can we do?' she asked. Now was the time to get to the edge of my comfort zone at that time. 'How about if I pray with you and the dog?' She agreed. I put my hand on the dog's back and said a prayer, for her and her husband as much as the dog. I can't remember the words. She seemed calmed by that. The most important thing was that someone had listened to her, taken her seriously and, I hope, affirmed her. I don't know if the dog 'got better', but I do know that, when I saw her in town a year or so later, she was neither bashful nor unhappy. Not a bad outcome.

That was an extreme encounter. More often, parents or adults seek baptism and we have to make sense of the sacrament to them, leaving them affirmed and certainly not damaged by their encounter with us. Our response will depend on our Church and our own understanding of baptism and, again, I do not intend to dictate the pathway you should take. What I will do is try to explore different scenarios and possibilities, highlighting the advantages and possible pitfalls of what we might do.

Adult or infant baptism?

For many, the policy of the Church, national or local, will determine which option is open to us. It can create a tension that, in those denominations offering choice, can be explored at a practical level. Looking at this will give those who have no choice some idea of the way forward in implementing the particular practice that is an option for them.

Looking at infant and adult baptism as options from a theological point of view, *Baptism, Eucharist and Ministry* (see the Resources section, under the heading 'Chapter 5', for full details) is invaluable. Though this has been with us for some years, it still gives a helpful analysis and underlines misunderstandings that may surround each practice.

At the outset, it should be stated that it is difficult to justify infant baptism from the New Testament, aside from the reference to the baptism of whole households. Even here it is disputable whether or not this would have included infants. Nevertheless, the practice of infant baptism has a long history and is the norm in many churches. In a book like this, we have to deal with what is, not with what might be. So, infant baptism, whatever its origin, is a fact. Those who baptize infants sometimes do so within a stringent framework requiring transparent commitment by the parents of the child. Others will be regarded as offering 'indiscriminate' baptism. The term 'indiscriminate' may sometimes be a true description of what is practised, but we should beware of labelling others without being aware of their understanding and practice.

Adult baptism may be regarded as more straightforward. We can trace the baptism of adults back to a number of New Testament sources – there is no difficulty in substantiating the practice. This does not mean that this form of baptism is immune from question or critique, however. The charge of exclusivism is sometimes addressed to those who follow this practice, but, in fact, many Baptists have a very open understanding of the incorporation of people into the Body of Christ and are welcoming to those who have been admitted in other ways in other denominations. Even those who are part of a 'closed' tradition may, in practice, be very open to others. Again, it is a case of ensuring that we do not criticize without first understanding. Often those who are most rigid in their application of creedal acceptance for baptism are those who have been or are operating in denominations that favour child baptism and are not happy with this themselves.

Questions in relation to infant baptism

For those baptizing infants, the first question that must be faced is 'What is baptism?' There is no single answer that will fit all those who uphold this practice so the list below may not be exhaustive. Again, what is important is that those who baptize infants should know and understand their own denomination or congregation's stance and be able to publicly justify their own position. If you cannot justify the practice, then you ought to ask how you will cope with integrity as a minister within your own particular denomination or congregation. So, what is baptism?

- An outward sign of God's forgiveness. If this is your understanding it raises questions as to the nature of sin. If you believe that we are born in sin and need God's grace from birth to forgive and protect us, then you will be comfortable with this perception. That, in turn, raises questions relating to personal responsibility for our actions.
- It incorporates people into the Body of Christ. If you are comfortable with this position, ask yourself if such incorporation requires any conscious action on the baby's part or is the intention of the parents sufficient?
- It demonstrates the Church's acceptance of children. If you believe this, is it a true representation of the congregation with whom you minister? In addition, does this recognition require water baptism or is it really a type of dedication?
- It represents God's acceptance of children. As with the last, if so, then does this recognition require water baptism or is it really a type of dedication?

In all cases we need to be sure of the role the parents have and what might happen at that stage when children are brought for baptism at an age when they are still the responsibility of their parents. Would this be children's or adults' baptism? The answer to this question may vary from one situation to another.

Practicalities relating to infant baptism

How immense your faith must be,
putting children in our hands.
Wonderful – the love you give;
trusting us with their demands.*

A parent telephones or approaches you to ask if you will baptize his or her child. How you respond to the request will depend on your answer to the questions above and the stance of your denomination or congregation.

A Local Ecumenical Partnership, comprising Baptist and United Reformed Church constituents, provides us with a model. The congregation was predominantly Baptist. If a parent requested infant baptism, which was the practice of the United Reformed part of the congregation, without any pejorative or weighted comment or judgment, the Baptist minister would refer the person to the partner United Reformed Church minister, who would then arrange the baptism. There was a clear recognition of the validity of this different practice.

This model helps us in the following way. If we are approached and asked to do something that, as an individual or representative of the Church, we cannot do, we need to recognize that we are being asked this by a fellow human being who is as worthy of God's love and our kindness as any other person. We may have contrary beliefs, but this first contact is not the time to air them. We need to know how we can respond in a way that maintains our integrity, our Church's discipline and yet is still pastorally sensitive to the person. Put another way, our response should leave the person feeling loved, welcomed and knowing that, in a different situation, he or she could turn to us again. To be able to refer to a colleague, even of another denomination, can be invaluable to you and to the wider mission of the Church.

If you are willing and able to baptize children, then you need to arrange to meet the parent(s). There has been a move towards classes involving groups of people, but, for those on the edge of the Church, individual personal contact can be less threatening and more constructive, so this should be offered if at all possible, though I am conscious that some denominations have a greater call for occasional services than others.

At the meeting, you can take down the necessary details about the child and parents in order to register the baptism. While there is no legal requirement to record baptisms, it is advisable to keep a register. Occasionally people will require proof of their baptism later in life, such as before marriage in some denominations or to attend a Church school. Careful record-keeping can help you or a successor to provide this information later if it is ever needed.

* Andrew Pratt. Reproduced by permission of Stainer & Bell Ltd.

Ask the parents what they understand by baptism. Always begin with them. They may have 'asked for the child to be done' or sought a 'christening'. However much you feel that they are using the wrong language or do not understand, resist the temptation to 'correct' them. Beware of the fact that they may be under pressure from other members of their family. This has to be what they want.

Listen carefully, then build on their understanding to lead them towards your or your Church's perception of baptism. They may say something like, 'It'll be best if the baby is baptized.' Ask them why and then build on the answer, talking about God, the Church or society valuing the child and that this can be a way of marking that. Underline their understanding of the importance of baptism. If this is their belief, baptism will incorporate the child into the Body of Christ. They need to know that what they think and do is important – that is why the parents make vows. You can see from these points why I stress the need to work individually. Different parents will be starting at different points of understanding. You will need to do more with some than others. Some will be more articulate than others. All need to be affirmed. You may need to arrange another meeting to discuss the next section.

Go over the order of service with them so that they know what to expect and what it all means. Ask the parents if there is anything or anyone they would like to be involved in the service. They may have a family member or friend who could sing or read or provide a poem. They could have a favourite song or even a lullaby that is special to them.

Trust them to choose the godparents. My godfather was an atheist, but my parents were allowed to choose him and he was very significant in my life. One of my son's godparents was chosen by the church. Three years after the baptism, we moved from the village and we've not been in touch since. It was no one's fault (or everyone's), but I know which model worked better!

Help them to 'own' the service. If possible meet or contact the parents again after they have had time to think.

Then there is the service itself. Different denominations will have different routines, different liturgies. As a rule of thumb, it is best for the baptism to take place as soon as possible in the service, especially if it is an 'ordinary' service and not one just for the baptism of infants. This reduces the stress for parents as they wait, wondering how long it will be before their child cries, if he or she isn't crying already!

Warm water is better than cold, though beware of giving the impression, with steam rising from the font on a cold day, that the child is going to be cooked! Even if someone else is responsible for putting water in the font and you trust him or her, always check that it really is there. You will be the one left holding the baby over an empty font if there is no water – it has happened!

Be confident and you will inspire confidence. If you haven't held a baby before, borrow a life-sized doll and practise, but, remember, real babies move! Enjoy this occasion and the family will enjoy it. This is one of the best opportunities for presenting the friendly face of the Church and opening up pastoral opportunities.

Summary

1. Know what you believe.
2. Accept the parents where they are.
3. They are not 'using' the Church – they came to you of their own free will, which is something we're always asking for.
4. Affirm them.
5. Help them to own the worship.
6. Enjoy the day and they will, too. They are also more likely to come back.
7. Keep good records.

Practicalities relating to adult baptism

Adult baptism is for those who can answer for themselves, so listen to those who are seeking baptism. There may be someone somewhere who has suggested that this is something they 'ought' to do. They may be under some peer or, more likely, parental pressure. Ensure that they really want to go through with this commitment themselves. It is easy to be swayed 'for a quiet life' or to go with the flow – 'everyone else is getting baptized, it seemed like the right thing to do'. This is a serious commitment by an individual in relation to God. The consequences of such a decision are more than simply a spiritual high. This should be the beginning of a lifelong commitment with no turning back. That needs to be underlined.

Get to know baptismal candidates. Hear their stories and testimonies. Understand not only why they want baptism but also what has brought them to this point. That way your response, in the present moment and your future pastoral care, will be more directly and helpfully focused. As you listen to what they are saying, prepare them by taking them from where they are by interpreting their experiences and calling in the context of the wider Church and the witness of the Bible.

Share the order of service with them, even if they have seen baptisms before. Participating is very different from observing. Adult baptism may be by sprinkling or full immersion. Particularly if it is the latter, take them to the baptistery and have a rehearsal.* Show them the way in which they will be baptized. This may be by lying back or lowering and ducking into the water. Take into account which is best for the candidate, given any disability or other issue, such as fear of water, that may present itself. Practise this as though they were being baptized for real so that they will know a little of what to expect when they are immersed. If there is likely to be a second person assisting, then it is good to involve that person, too.

Answer candidates' questions as best you can, however naive they may seem to be. For them, the questions are important. This may be something you have done regularly, but, for them, it is the first and only time.

On the day, ensure that those who are assisting and supporting know what their roles are and trust them. If this is your first time officiating, don't be afraid to ask for help and advice. However solemn this time may be, it is immensely significant and also joyful for the candidate. Let them enjoy it and enjoy it with them.

> So we go to all the world,
> a rising, praising people.
> We're not content to be confined
> by liturgy or steeple.
> God is calling, we're responding,
> lives are for the giving,
> stepping out we trust God's grace,
> our lives are for the living.**

As mentioned above, but it's easy to forget at this point, keep careful records so that you or your successor can produce evidence of baptism at a later date should this be needed.

There is an addendum to this. As full immersion baptism is practised on people professing their faith, it is important to ask the question, how do we approach baptism of people who have learning difficulties? Are we to exclude them or do we work at their level of understanding and leave the rest to God? If you are following the spirit of this book, you will choose the latter option. If you do, be prepared, if necessary, to articulate your reasons to your congregation, with due sensitivity to those seeking baptism. Whatever you say and however you behave, imagine yourself in the place of those you are

*Invariably this would be a dry run. Most baptisteries take a long time to fill and many hours to heat.
** Andrew Pratt. Reproduced by permission of Stainer & Bell Ltd.

baptizing and ask, 'Would I like to be spoken of or treated like this?' Don't make any presumptions that they are unable to understand. They may have a better grasp of what you are thinking than you could ever know.

Confirmation – a note

Historically baptism and confirmation were one and the same rite. Different denominations regard confirmation differently and provide appropriate liturgies for it. In terms of preparation for those seeking confirmation, the process sould be the same as that for those asking for adult baptism, with the obvious differences relating to the practicalities associated with each rite.

Summary

1. Get to know the baptismal candidates.
2. Listen to their stories.
3. Help them to make this occasion special and personal to them.
4. Be sensitive to people with different levels of understanding and ways of expressing their faith.
5. Keep careful records.

Looking ahead

- Remember that every request you receive for baptism is an opportunity to share God's love and grace.
- What does 'using the Church' mean?
- Is this something people ever really do?

Note

- Remember that every request you receive for baptism is an opportunity to share God's love and grace.
- What does 'using the Church' mean?
- Is this something that people ever really do?

Chapter 6
Communion – making the presence real

The holy stuff of life,
these ordinary things,
become a means of sacrament,
a blessing that God brings.

We take the bread and wine,
remember that last meal,
re-live again a fated night
to make Christ's presence real.

'Minister, we want to have Communion at our next house group. Is that all right?' As the minister I wouldn't be there, but, although it is not the church in the sense of the building, it is in the sense of the people. For some, the answer would be 'yes', for some 'no' or OK between consenting adults in private! If they hadn't asked, I would not have known.

In the notices it said, 'Lord's Supper', but no minister had been appointed to lead the service, only worship leaders who, in the denomination concerned, were not ordained. Should I stay or should I go? Someone suggested that a minister would probably have consecrated the bread and wine beforehand. Would that work? For some certainly. For others it raises profound questions about the nature and theology of Communion.

The fact that, in some churches, these questions can be raised indicates how hazy people's understanding of Communion can be. For most, the denomination or congregation will have expectations, if not rules, about such things. Increasingly, individuals, even in denominations with formal structures, will ask what is allowed in a house group or outside of the ordinary structures of worship. For this reason, we need to know what the strictures are within which we work and what is possible without going against our own integrity. We must start by being sure of what we believe and knowing what church law is for our particular denomination.

The nature of Communion

The different names by which Communion is known is a good starting point for exploring its nature.

The Mass

This carries with it a sense of sacrifice and relates Communion to temple worship. Each time the Mass takes place, a sacrifice is offered again. This can be underlined by the use of a 'mixed chalice'. When the elements are prepared both wine and water are added to one chalice to recollect that:

> when they came to Jesus and saw that he was already dead, they did not break his legs. Instead, one of the soldiers pierced his side with a spear, and at once blood and water came out.

(John 19.33–34)

The idea of an altar makes sense for those with this understanding as it is furniture used for sacrifice. The priest stands in Jesus' stead. At the point of consecration – the epiclesis – the bread and wine become literally the body and blood of Christ. This is not the place to examine in detail the theology of the nature of this transubstantiation, but what is important to note here, in an ecumenical context, is that, for many, this is a reality and of crucial significance. The prayer asking that the bread and wine become the body and blood is critical and it is sometimes accompanied by the ringing of a bell to indicate the actual moment of consecration.

If the bread and wine really are the body and blood of Christ, then the handling and disposal of these elements requires extra care. At the end of Communion, all the bread and wine that has been consecrated must either be consumed or kept as reserved sacrament – that is, bread and wine that has been already consecrated. This can be used in Communion and distributed by an authorized layperson to, for instance, the sick. The manner in which the Communion vessels are cleaned is also critical, even to the point of there being a basin in the sacristy (vestry) with a drain that goes straight to earth and not to a sewer. It goes without saying that careless disposal of the elements would be regarded as sacrilegious. The whole liturgy is therefore often, though need not be, solemn as a mark of respect.

The reality of the transformation of the bread and wine into the body and blood of Christ is further underlined by the liturgy of Benediction. In this service, the consecrated bread is venerated as the body of Christ.

The Eucharist

The word 'Eucharist' literally means thanksgiving and comes from the Greek word for thanks used at the Last Supper: 'he took a loaf of bread, and when he had given thanks . . .' (Luke 22.19). There is a sense of joy in this word that is not always obvious in the acts of worship known as the Eucharist. That having been said, central to such an act is the anaphora – the great prayer of thanksgiving – that in most formal liturgies precedes the words of institution, the retelling of the Last Supper. Just as the epiclesis is critical in the Mass, so the prayer of thanksgiving is essential to the Eucharist. Without these words of thanksgiving, there is no Eucharist. The form of the words may vary, but usually they encompass an understanding of God as creator and Jesus as saviour or redeemer. For these, thanks is given. The bread, as in the Mass, is broken as a separate action after the Communion prayers.

The Lord's Supper

As the name suggests, this form of Communion looks back to the Last Supper and understands the present worship as emulating the meal that Jesus shared with his disciples. For some, this is not unlike the Eucharist and may share all the same elements. There can be a prayer of thanksgiving, the words of institution and even an epiclesis. In this form, the bread will be broken after these parts of the service have been recited.

That having been said, the very name hints that there is room for flexibility here. While the service may follow a traditional form and structure, it might equally have no epiclesis or prayer of thanksgiving and the bread may be broken during the recitation of the Words of Institution. It is not uncommon for these words to be read in context from the New Testament. The intention is to emulate the words of the Last Supper as closely and as scripturally as possible. There is less emphasis here on what is happening to the bread and wine and more on recalling the narrative of Scripture. It is therefore more appropriate to use the term 'table' instead of 'altar'.

Communion

This is less a way of sharing the meal and more an understanding of what happens during the meal from a metaphysical perspective or in terms of its symbolism for the relationship between the participants and God and each other.

In the Old Testament, Moses took the blood of oxen and poured some over an altar and the rest over the people (Exodus 24.5–8). This was to symbolize a covenant made between God and the people. In the same way, Communion is rooted in the idea that there can be a close association between God and people. The essence of Communion also carries with it the human understanding that sharing a meal with others confers acceptance of them and offers a bond between them. So, as bread and wine are shared, for some there is an affirmation of communion with God but also of fellowship with the other participants.

A further meaning comes from the Pauline theology of the body of Christ, that all the people of the Church together make up the body of Christ. Sharing the meal is a way of making this concept of the body visible and real. Here, people from many different backgrounds meet and share. Together they are one, but there is also an underlying understanding that each is valuable and has a particular place at the table. For some this is evidence of the equality of all people. In this case, Communion may well be celebrated 'in the round', with no 'head of the table', the communicants serving each other.

Remembrance

For some, this is the most important of the possible emphases. The word comes from the Greek word 'anamnesis', which, strictly speaking, means a putting together in the present of something that took place in the past, hence 're-membering'.

So, it is far more than simply recollection and means that, in the process of the worship, Jesus is present and those who share do so in the same way that the first disciples shared. This may simply be an understanding brought to mind by the words 'we do this in remembrance . . .', but some will want to take this further by describing the Last Supper in a fuller way than is usual, using more than just the Words of Institution. Others will seek to re-enact the meal in a dramatic way. For some there is an eschatological emphasis, for we 'proclaim the Lord's death until he comes'.

Other approaches

Against this panorama, it is also important to not forget that the Salvation Army and the Society of Friends who, while not using sacraments in the way other Christian denominations do, are not anti-sacramentalist. Their position is better characterized as being pan-sacramentalist, in that all things are seen as being potentially sacramental. Bread was broken and thanks given at every Jewish meal in Jesus' day. This gives us the authority to regard every ordinary meal as sacramental.

It must also be remembered that Communion may be celebrated daily, weekly or as infrequently as annually.

If you have been brought up in a single denomination, this plethora of interpretations and modes of practice may seem both overwhelming and irrelevant. For your own worship in your own church, this wider view is not essential. Nevertheless, it provides two important elements of value:

1. If you understand the practices of other Christians, you are less likely to cause them offence.
2. This wider view may enable you, either through practice, teaching or simply by your own understanding, to approach Communion in ways that are innovative or more meaningful for your congregation. In this, however, you should always be sensitive to the expectations of the people with whom you minister.

Come with joy to offer worship,
meet your neighbour face to face,
offer her the hand of greeting,
share this fountain of God's grace.
Bring the bread of loving kindness,
channel love to heart and mind,
bringing glory to this meeting,
calm and comforting and kind.

Bring the wine of celebration
to this eucharistic feast;
where all gifts and lives are welcome
where each person finds release.
Handle myst'ries, make them friendly,
join together, offer prayer;
live the meaning of your singing,
seeing Christ in all who share.*

Practicalities

Whatever stance you take, whatever the theology of your congregation in relation to Communion, it is appropriate that you act with dignity. This does not mean that you are rigid, austere or lacking in humour. It does mean that you recognize the worship in which you are involved is significant – perhaps more than usually significant. How you express this may be in your manner, your language or the way you dress.

At the table

For formal liturgies, the altar or table should always be prepared in a way that makes it look tidy, even elegant. Take time over this. If you have others who are involved in the preparation, take time to encourage them, affirm them and thank them for a job well done.

Make sure that the altar frontal, if there is one, is neatly placed. Communion linen, it goes without saying, should be clean. If purificators (linen cloths for wiping the chalice) are used, these should be freshly laundered. The Communion pieces – the cruet, chalice, paten (if these are used) or the trays of cups and plate – should be placed neatly. If the chalice and paten are covered by a burse, take time to make this attractive and symmetrical in appearance. If a plain linen cloth covers the elements, then, equally, this should be placed neatly.

* Andrew Pratt. Reproduced by permission of Stainer & Bell Ltd.

When handling the Communion ware, be careful. Practise this beforehand. If a cruet is used, be sure that you can pour without spilling and can reach all the items that you need to before the service begins.

When handling a chalice, determine what is local practice. Do people expect to take the chalice from the officiant or do they anticipate that it will be placed to their lips. Do all or any expect intincture – that is, to take the bread and wait to dip it in the wine or for the officiant to do this for them? Do members of the congregation assist in the distribution of the elements?

If trays of glasses are used, ensure that you know what to do in the event that there are not enough to go round. Again, practise with the trays. Sometimes trays are made to stack. If this is the case, find out beforehand how they unstack. It has been known for two trays to be picked up together and for the bottom one to drop away clear of the Communion table. Find out what happens to empty glasses. Is there a rail with holders or must they be collected? Again, find out if stewards have been appointed to share in the distribution of the elements and who, in local practice, is acceptable in this role.

Find out what the logistics are in terms of people receiving Communion. This can vary from place to place and even from one occasion to another in the same place. A single or double row of people may present themselves to be served and afterwards return to their seats. People may come as they are bid by stewards or of their own volition. Some may stand or kneel at a Communion rail and go after being served. Others will not leave until a brief dismissal prayer has been said. Still others will wait in their seats to be served. Also, if people are coming forward, how do you know when the last person has come forward? This may seem obvious, but it is easy to miss either someone sitting in a pew waiting to be served or the last person coming slowly forward. You can be assisted in this by agreeing with a steward who will keep a watch and then come up last. Then you know that when he or she has received, you have definitely finished.

It is well to know what is going to happen before you begin. If it goes wrong, it will reflect on you!

What to wear
This will obviously depend on the expectations of the church or denomination in which you serve. Some Anglican churches will provide a cope or chasuble that may well match the altar frontal and other falls or drapes. You will most likely need to provide your own alb, cassock and surplice. Those churches where less formal dress is expected will anticipate that the minister will provide this. Whatever you wear, remember that, even if what you choose is very informal, the moment it is used in a liturgical setting, it becomes

'liturgical dress'. Attempts to 'dress down' can be gimmicky, so beware. If what you are wearing is formal, take care and don't simply assume that a cassock will cover a multitude of 'sins'. If the cassock is black, for instance, then black trousers and shoes make sense and look right.

Remember that what you wear may signify your role, but it is not there to draw unwarranted attention to you.

What to say

This may be determined by the accepted or stipulated liturgical practice of your denomination or congregation. The main rule here is to remember that, while you may know your way around the book or books you are using, even some of the regular members of the congregation may not. They will soon let you know if you are announcing page or paragraph numbers too often! Even then, visitors may find it helpful.

Where there is a choice, there are a few rules of thumb worth considering.

- If you enquire how Communion is conducted, you may well be told, 'In the usual way'. Ask what this is. What you understand as normal may be very different from what your congregation expects.
- Do not change things more than you would simply as a consequence of 'you being you' without asking yourself why you are making the change.
- Explain any changes you make so that you take the congregation with you. For instance, their practice may have been to have small cubes of bread and you may prefer to use a roll that can be broken at the blessing. Tell them why you want to do this.
- In a church that is free to use written or extempore liturgies, ring the changes so there is some variety and the needs and wants of different people are met.
- If a complete departure from the regular practice of the congregation is planned, it is best to give notice and explanation beforehand. It may all be clear to you, but could be unsettling to those with whom you minister.

For those who have the opportunity to be creative with the liturgy, then judicious use of drama, dance, light and data projection can be greatly beneficial. If you go down this route, don't overdo it and don't allow the way you present the sacrament to be predictable in the sense of the congregation expecting a particular style of presentation because you are there. Creating new liturgies has the intention of refreshing practice, but, predictability, even in terms of the use of a particular type of technology, can mitigate against this.

When it's all over

The elements should be disposed of reverently and sensitively, bearing in mind the expectations of those with whom you serve. The worship space should be left in a way that the next person using it has to make the minimum of effort in order to do so. In other words, leave the place as you would expect to find it!

Summary

1. Find out what the local practices are and follow them unless there is good reason to do otherwise.
2. Take care over what you wear.
3. Practise what you are going to do.
4. Find out, as far as you can, what others are likely to do.

Looking ahead

*   Learn from what others do.
*   Reflect on all the things that Communion can be and let this inform your practice.
*   Be appropriately creative.

Chapter 7
Marriage and civil partnerships

A disparate group of people were gathered in the modern town-centre church. There was some uncomfortable shuffling. The culture and the context were strange. Some young girls giggled while a few of the young men had drunk rather more than they might usually have done by one o'clock in the afternoon. Nevertheless, they were going to do this right. The tailcoats and the hat worn by the bride's mother spoke of effort and concern.

The congregation was welcomed. A hymn was sung – 'All things bright and beautiful' as the bride vaguely remembered it from her school days. 'Is there any just cause or reason . . .?' There was a slight shuffling of feet, looking over shoulders, the odd childish grin. The wedding proceeded, the congregation listened to the address and another bashful couple were proclaimed man and wife. I was about to say, though I don't always, 'You may kiss the bride', when a bridesmaid leant forward and, in something more than a stage whisper, called along the front row to the bride, 'Go on, give him a good snog!' You never know quite what will happen at a wedding!

So what is marriage for?

You may have a number of answers to this question in your mind, but it is worth looking back culturally and historically to what has formed the view of marriage that is upheld by law and custom in this country.

Archaic though this may seem, I want to begin with the *Book of Common Prayer*. There are echoes here of what Augustine said in the fifth century, but even that is not the real starting point. Marriage was a social institution long before Christianity and it was far too important for Christians to ignore.

However marriage is seen today, our views and laws have been formed and have then evolved from this starting point.

There are three elements that are recognized here:

1. It was ordained for the procreation of children, to be brought up in the fear and nurture of the Lord, and to the praise of his holy Name.
2. It was ordained as a remedy against sin, and to avoid fornication; that such persons as have not the gift of continency might marry, and keep themselves undefiled members of Christ's body.

3.   It was ordained for the mutual society, help, and comfort, that the one ought to have of the other, both in prosperity and adversity.

To begin with, the *Book of Common Prayer* talks of the procreation of children. There were social and biological reasons for beginning at this point. The theological stress here was secondary. The next criterion was that of a defence against sin. It was understood that people were tempted to have intercourse with each other and outside of marriage this was regarded as fornication. Therefore, marriage was intended to prevent this sin. Finally, it was stated that marriage was for the mutual support of a man and a woman and, in spite of the date of this document, there is a surprising sense of equality of responsibility envisaged between the partners.

It is unlikely that most couples seeking marriage today, particularly those without any formal religious affiliation, would envisage applying these criteria to their own situation. Regarding the first, many children are brought up by people who are not married and, however much the Church and certain political moralists would want to argue for the priority of marriage, society runs counter to this in practice if not in belief. Many children are brought up by a single parent or by parents who live apart.

The second criterion, to prevent sin, would only be upheld by a very small proportion of the population as, in our society, generally intercourse before marriage is, if not the norm, highly prevalent.

The last aspect, that of mutual support, for which we use the shorthand 'love', is likely to be the first reason a couple gives for seeking marriage.

Societal norms have changed and, however much the Church may regret that, it is the context in which we live. It has profound consequences for those who minister within the Church.

If we are to seek to apply the first criteria, does it mean that we should refuse marriage to or see it as inappropriate for couples who, for whatever reason, could not or did not want to have children? Do we have the power to refuse marriage to anyone who has had intercourse outside of marriage? If so, how rigorously are we willing to question people to determine whether or not they meet our standards?

As to the last suggestion, that marriage is for mutual support, does this mean that we should alter the liturgy to remove things that suggest symbolically marriage is an unequal relationship in which a woman is a possession of her father's until she is is passed to her husband, such as the bride being 'given away' or the wearing of a ring.

Like so many other aspects of the life of the Church and its ministry, marriage asks fundamental questions of our theology and our own honesty and integrity. This has been illustrated most clearly in the last 25 years as people in gay and lesbian relationships, no longer illegal, have sought their affirmation in law and through the Church.

The argument has been made that the key aspect of any relationship, formal or informal, is that it offers mutual respect and support. If this is so in marriage, then procreation becomes secondary. Unless we are willing to rigorously question heterosexual couples, then the question of sexual relations in lesbian or gay ones becomes secondary to what has been called 'co-creativity' – the building up of one another in security and trust. If this is so, it is argued, homosexual relationships have the potential to be every bit as valid as heterosexual ones.

Whether your view is that the Bible allows for this or not will depend on your attitude to biblical interpretation and authority. For some, such relationships will always be anathema; for others they are acceptable. Still others will will be uncertain. Whatever our personal views, as in all of our pastoral relationships, we need to be able to operate within the constraints of Church law, the law of the land and our own integrity while recognizing the common humanity of those with whom and to whom we minister.

> Love joins our hearts and minds as one,
> Love shares our grief, our joy, our fun,
> Love works, love's work is never done,
> Love always lives.*

Pastoral questions

A couple sat with me in my house. They wanted to get married. Before coming to see me, the woman had telephoned and asked, 'We want to get married, but my fiancé has been married before. Is that all right?' I simply agreed to talk with them.

At that time, my Church regulations stated that, in the case of second (or subsequent) marriages, the officiating minister had to interview the couple and, regarding the person who had been through divorce, determine who had been at fault. No decision was to be given to the couple at that point as to whether they could be married in a church or not. The content of the interview was then to be shared with a senior colleague and a decision made. All that could then be communicated to the couple was that the Church would or would not marry them.

So, the couple sat there and we talked. I have to say, I had serious misgivings. When I saw my senior colleague, I shared this with him. 'Then you must not marry them,' was his response. I duly communicated this to the

* Andrew Pratt. Reproduced by permission of Stainer & Bell Ltd.

couple, who wanted to know on what grounds they had 'been rejected'. I had no answer and said so, simply that the Church would not marry them. They were upset and angry. I never saw them again.

All of this bothered me and, a few months later, I was talking with a minister of another denomination. He was older and wiser than me and I am still grateful for what he shared. He asked me what that couple would do next – would they not get married, then? I said that they almost certainly would get married. 'Where?' he asked. 'A register office' was my response. Very gently he asked me who would support them there. It was obvious that, with the best will in the world, register offices are not set up to provide support and counselling. He asked me if they would go to church. Not very likely. He then pressed me as to why I had made my decision. It was a gut reaction masked with dubious theology. I hardly knew the couple, didn't know their background and I had judged them on the strength of one interview and my feelings.

He then asked a 'crunch question'. 'If they had been getting married for the first time, would you have felt any different?' I had to answer 'No'. 'Would you have refused them marriage?' Within my Church law I would have had no grounds whatever to refuse them in that situation.

My colleague was very gentle with me. 'Don't you think that you may have missed an opportunity there, to care, to support? Perhaps they were very hurt before they even met you. I don't think you'll have made them feel much better.' He might have added that I'd also single-handedly lost them to the Church.

All of this made me think very hard. Obviously we either have to abide by the laws of our Church or challenge them in appropriate ways. We also have to keep the integrity of our own faith.

When people come to us seeking marriage, it is always a pastoral if not an evangelistic opportunity. Those who have been married before may have suffered damaged trust and be subject to self-doubt. They may have been physically or psychologically abused. They may have married young or been forced into marriage because of their own norms or those of others.

Whatever judgement we may need to make, we should make it with understanding and with a view to all the consequences. This is very much a case of asking 'How would I feel if this was me?' It is also a time for realism. If I was divorced and seeking remarriage, if I was being interviewed by a minister who could decide for or against that marriage, I hope that I would not lie, but I might well be economical with the truth. I would say the things that I thought would have a positive outcome for me.

In order to make this sort of decision about someone's future, we need to build a relationship of trust with them, to know them well. If you have to decide at the end of a half-hour or even an hour-long interview, at least be realistic enough to admit that your decision will be made according to Church law or prejudice and rarely from an informed position, one of understanding the couple's situation. In that light, ask yourself how best that couple can leave you affirmed as a result of meeting with you and still open to the Church's ministry.

A colleague telephoned. He'd just moved into the area. He was aware that I was able and willing to perform weddings for people who had been married before. 'It's like this,' he said, 'in conscience I can't take on such weddings and I wondered if I might refer anyone on to you?' I said that was all right and asked how we might do this. 'Oh well, if someone approaches me, I'll tell them that I don't believe in remarriage, that it is wrong, but if they still want to go ahead . . .'. I stopped him. 'Look,' I said, 'if people have been through divorce, there's a chance that they're already damaged enough without you telling them that they're in the wrong, too. If you want to pass people to me, that's fine, but just say that you can't marry them and give them my number.' We have our own consciences to contend with, but that does not allow us to put others down without knowing their circumstances.

Be prepared

A lot has been said about the preparation of people for marriage and the Church's role and responsibility in this. What I will set out here is an ideal, but it is an ideal that has worked for me. You may need to modify the approach depending on your own position and that of your denomination or congregation.

The first contact
Usually you will receive a phone call, sometimes you will be approached face to face. 'We want to get married. Are you able to marry us?' They may volunteer the fact that they have not been married before or that one or other of the partnership has. If you are in a position to proceed, make an appointment to meet face to face reasonably soon, even if the wedding is to be a year or two away. The couple have approached you and, even if you have no need to make any plans at this point, they may well have. Don't sneer at the fact that a venue for a reception may need to be booked two years ahead – just be glad it's not your problem and don't hold them up.

The first meeting (see also Preparation – some details on p. 65)
This is the point at which you can begin to work formally with the couple and indicate what is ahead for them. Take down all the information you will need for registration purposes. If you are in the Church of England, you will act as *de facto* registrar for all the processes involved. In other denominations, the

local registrar of births, marriages and deaths will be involved – more about this later. In either case, it is wise to take down full names, addresses, occupations, ages, marital status and the names and occupations of the bride and groom's fathers. These last two can be dealt with sensitively. Historically, the information was used for identification. Not everyone knows their father's, or even their mother's name, however, and there is no legal requirement for these to be recorded, though there is space for them on the register.

Determine the date of the wedding and inform them of any fees that will be charged and what these will cover. If the date of the wedding is a long way ahead, either fix the cost or let them know of any potential increase that is likely to affect them.

Tell the couple what the legal requirements are in terms of registration of the wedding. Now set the scene for what is to follow in terms of preparation and then answer any questions they may have.

Set the date of the next meeting. If the wedding is a long way off, this can be suitably delayed. The important thing is that the couple should be secure in the knowledge that their wedding is going ahead, things have been set in motion and they can contact you again if they need to know anything else in the interim.

The second meeting
This is an opportunity to go through the wedding liturgy in detail and inform the couple of any choices that are possible in terms of the words, music and so on.

The third meeting
At this meeting, the couple sets out what they want for the wedding day in detail.

The fourth meeting
This is the time for a wedding practice. Set this a short time before the big day – near enough to be remembered, yet with enough time to allow for last-minute adjustments that may be necessary.

Let the bride and groom bring whoever they wish to this meeting. The bride's mother or the best man may be more nervous than the main participants! This gives time for them to ask questions about a role that is significant for them.

The wedding day – some practicalities

Registration
The legal requirements for marriage in England and Wales (in Scotland, the regulations are different) apply only to heterosexual relationships (civil partnerships are discussed separately below). For those in the Church of

England, you are most likely to be guided through the necessary legalities and practicalities during your curacy. In other denominations, you may find yourself well or less well supported.

It must be noted that the legal requirements relating to marriage in England and Wales have been under review for some time, so it is important that you ensure you comply with the requirements in force at the time of any weddings you perform. The requirements will probably change within the lifetime of this book.

At the time of writing, you are likely to be appointed as an 'authorized person'.* This is an appointment made by the managing body of your church – your church council, for instance – and this body will need to apply to the General Register Office to enable this to happen. Ideally, this will be done for you, but do check that it has, especially if a wedding has been booked to take place soon after you have been newly appointed. On appointment, you will be given a book of guidelines that set out all you need to know. Each registered building should have a register and the paperwork necessary to allow you to make returns to the local registrar.

When a couple are going to get married, they should book the date with you and then contact the local registrar (the possibility of registering online is being explored, but, at the time of writing, is not in use for marriages, though it is for civil partnerships). The registrar, at the appropriate time, will complete two certificates – one for each person – that will be displayed at the register office to give notice of the intended marriage. These certificates will later be given to the couple who should give them to you ahead of the wedding day. When you get them, check all the details with the couple and against the information you took from them at your first meeting. If there are any discrepancies, however small, contact the registrar and ask how he or she wants you to deal with them. The registrar may produce new certificates or ask for a pencil amendment. Asking in this way means that you comply with what is required by law as understood by the registrar who will be dealing with you as, in effect, an agent. Registrars will always be willing to help and support you. Use their expertise.

The information on the certificates is what you use to fill in the registers on the day of the wedding. Legally, the registers – there are two – should not be completed until the couple have made their vows, which are, in effect, the legal contract of marriage between them. Before the registers are signed, have the bride and groom check them. If any alteration is required, refer to

---

* There are sometimes exceptions to this and, for instance, the Baptist Union advice is that it should not be the minister who is appointed, this role being filled by a lay person. In this case the minister would conduct the service, while the authorized person would have to attend and deal with legal matters such as registration.

the guidelines you have been given – there are legally recognized ways of altering these documents. If you are in any doubt, contact the registrar at the earliest opportunity. The registrar is there to help in this way and will prefer a question than having to untangle your mistakes later.

The marriage certificate that is issued to the couple should be an exact copy of the entry in the registers. At the end of each quarter, a copy of the entries is made on a sheet provided for the purpose by the registrar. If any building has no weddings within a quarter, a nil return is made, also on a document provided by the registrar.

Before you agree a wedding, perhaps even before you have one booked, it is a good idea to use one of the return sheets to fill in an imaginary wedding to practise what you have to do. You can check how to do this as you go against the authorized person's guidelines so that you are not doing it for the first time at the first wedding.

Preparation – some details

What I am going to suggest involves an individual approach, but it takes seriously the fact that every relationship is different and all people have different histories that have made them who they are.

The method of preparation that I use is exactly the same whether I am preparing a young couple who have never been married, people who have been divorced or an older couple who may have been widowed.

Begin by making clear that we all have a background. We may or may not have had other relationships than the one being sealed by this marriage. Explain that the order of service can be used not just as a preparation for the wedding day, but to ask questions of each other that might not yet have been asked. If, within your denomination, it is possible to alter or adapt the liturgy, make it clear that, while there is a format that can be followed, the couple can make it their own. So, if the liturgy mentions the upbringing of children, you can illustrate that, for some, this might not be appropriate and the words can be missed out. Similarly, what does it mean to speak of the union of one man and one woman for life when there has been a divorce? What issues of trust are lurking here? Leave the couple to explore. Let them know that you are willing to talk with them about any issues they uncover, but that you are not seeking to pry.

When you apply this approach what happens? Let me give you an example.

We were meeting for the third time. 'Before we go any further, can we just talk about something', she said. I was sitting with two people in their forties. Both had been divorced and had children from their previous marriages. 'It's just that we keep arguing, falling out. We love each other, but with all this we're not sure it's right to get married. Can we at least postpone it?' I agreed that that was sensible and asked if they wanted to talk about the situation. They did.

Cutting a long story short, after several monthly meetings, they discovered that what was happening was that, when he saw his children, he saw his ex-partner and his new partner was jealous. The same thing happened, but in reverse, when she saw her children. A year on, I asked if they still loved one another. They did. I asked if the situation with wanting to see the children would change. It wouldn't. Could they cope now they understood what was happening, though? They thought they could. So I asked if they'd like to get married. They did.

None of this came out of my asking questions of them, but of them asking questions of themselves and having somewhere safe to talk through the answers. If I'd refused to marry them, that opportunity would have been lost.

Another couple had just turned 20, never been married before and one of them was a member of my church, whose family came to the church. They came to me for their third meeting.

'We have something we need to share before we get started.' I asked what it was. 'We don't love each other, but what can we tell Dad – he's already booked the reception?'

Knowing how young people's feelings can swing about, I asked how they felt about each other. They were straight with me. Having read the order of service, it had made them think. They liked each other, respected each other, but marriage demanded more than this.

So, the young woman told her father, who was relieved that he was hearing this now and not after the wedding. Two years later, she married 'Mr Right'. Dad was grateful. He told me so.

I offer these illustrations to demonstrate the way in which this type of preparation can be effective with those entering a first or second marriage as a tool to help them ask questions of each other that it would be impertinent of me, an outsider, to ask and to which I would be unlikely to get an honest answer.

The liturgy
Each denomination or congregation will have an order of service for a wedding. In some circumstances your Church may expect you to use this service without alteration. If you are able to be flexible, then, bearing in mind that some parts are a legal necessity for the marriage, you can allow the couple to be creative with the rest of the liturgy.

Obviously you will need to be comfortable with what they suggest. As minister, you have a right of veto. For that reason, do not raise the couple's expectations and then say that they cannot have what they have planned.

If you do feel able to offer them the possibility of preparing their own service, the outcome can be very creative and personal. Examples include liturgies or just vows written by the couples themselves that express exactly what they want to say and not what the Church is telling them that they must say. Different cultural or linguistic elements can be incorporated. I have been involved in Anglo-Tongan and Anglo-French acts of worship. Different members of the family may have skills that can be incorporated – writing, singing, playing a musical instrument. If the bride has no father or is older, she may appreciate walking into the church with her husband-to-be.

The permutations are as infinite as the personalities who come to be married. Each is different and each is special. At one extreme, I have officiated at weddings with much pomp, circumstance and ceremony, while, at the other, I conducted a marriage between two people, one of whom was on licence from prison, with no hymns and just seven people present, including myself, the organist and a church steward.

Civil partnerships and same-sex relationships

The tangent, the touching, where God warms each heart
provides re-creation, we make a new start
for here love is grounded and grace can be found;
for here God speaks quietly and whispers resound.

Different denominations and congregations are offering various guidelines as to how or if civil partnerships and same-sex relationships are to be handled. Clearly, if this is an area in which you feel called to work and your denomination or congregation are accepting of it, then the main thing to recognize is that, in law, what is being addressed, though similar to marriage, is not marriage. To my knowledge, at the present time, authorized persons cannot conduct civil partnership ceremonies. By and large, the Church is not pressing for this – it has enough difficulty accepting the concept of same-sex relationships as it is.

The procedure in terms of registering for a civil partnership is much the same as that for marriage. Registration can take place online, but the partners still have to visit the registrar prior to the ceremony. Within the ceremony, there need be no vows and the partnership is sealed by the signing of a schedule.

If you are in a position to offer people blessings or you are approached for this, the first criterion must be that the event should be affirming of the people concerned. It is unacceptable, but a matter of fact, that the blessing of a gay couple could cause unpleasantness in many congregations. If this is the case where you are, think of the couple being blessed and do not subject them to a situation that would mar their day – better to find another venue. As the blessing of a same-sex relationship is not a legal matter, it can take place anywhere. If the couple want a church, ensure that it is 'friendly'. If not, many hotels are willing to make premises available and, unlike a civil marriage, there are no restrictions on the religious language used.

All these issues aside, the same comments that I have made in relation to preparation and liturgy are equally applicable here. There are increasing quantities of resources in terms of liturgies, prayers and hymns suitable for these occasions.

Summary

1. Be prepared.
2. If you are an authorized person, make a friend of your local registrar. He or she is there to help you.
3. Be sensitive to the people with whom you are dealing.
4. Those who have been through broken relationships may carry a burden of guilt and self-doubt. Don't add to it.
5. Treat those who are involved in same-sex partnerships with the same sensitivity and consideration as everyone else. Do I need to say that? Unfortunately, I think that I do, even, or perhaps especially, within the Church.
6. You may have performed many weddings. Treat each one as if it were the most important.

Looking ahead

- Allow time for weddings.
- Allow time for people to be late.
- However you feel, enable the people present to celebrate.

Chapter 8
Death and bereavement

It was a small church with a central isle. At most it would have seated 40 or 50, I suppose. It was packed to the doors, with a few people standing in the vestibule. She had been popular and the whole family, friends and neighbours had turned out to mourn her passing, to celebrate her life.

The organ was the sort that could have graced a pub or club as easily as a chapel. The organist had been asked to play before the funeral, but then turn on some recorded music when the coffin was due to be brought in. He was poised, ready, having turned round on the organ stool to face into the body of the church. The music that had been chosen was popular, but suitably solemn for the occasion. The undertaker appeared and nodded. The congregation rose. The organist hit the button. From the small player came the music, loudly, with a strong beat . . . 'O happy day!' The organist had never moved so fast before. He hit the stop button, swung his legs over the organ stool and struck up 'Abide with me' as though this was utterly routine.

Things don't always go as you've planned!

Trying to be prepared

I had been appointed to my very first church. In two weeks I was to be inducted. I'd travelled 100 miles to the house where I was going to live to do one or two things before moving in. It was a warm day, midsummer, all the windows were open. I was halfway up a ladder, paintbrush in hand, when the phone rang. The voice on the other end asked if I was the minister. Well I was, sort of. The other minister had moved. 'So will you do a funeral, then?' For that I needed to be prepared.

How do you prepare? Like so many other situations in ministry, you can never be totally prepared. Events can throw the most experienced minister. What you can do is do your best to know yourself and those things that make you vulnerable. That's a start. After my son had been killed in an accident at the age of 22, I had to be careful for some time to ensure that funerals of young people were conducted by a colleague. Eight years on, I still have to be careful as I listen to the stories of bereaved parents to use my knowledge to help me empathize, not use them to minister to my grief.

Now that sort of event is stark, obvious. It is the hidden griefs we carry, though, that can sometimes jump out and surprise us, making it more difficult to minister helpfully and effectively to those who mourn. We need a way to alert ourselves to as many of these as we can so that we are at least aware of some of our areas of vulnerability.

Begin by putting together a timeline for your life. On it, mark significant events that are positive and others that are negative.

1. How do these events make you feel?
2. You have remembered all of them. Ask yourself why they are still significant.
3. What is the most negative thing that has happened that is still having an influence within your life?
4. How would you feel if you were confronted by someone who had had a similar experience?
5. Does your experience enable you to empathize or does it disable you?
6. Do you feel that you could listen to them, to hear their story, or would you need to interject to share your story?

If you are able to work through this sort of questioning in confidence with a colleague, you will gain even greater insight. That colleague must be someone you can trust, though, and what you divulge to each other must be kept in confidence.

It is important to acknowledge any unresolved issues that surface via this process.

While doing this with a group of students, I was taken to task for not warning them that this process might be painful and they might wish to walk out partway through. That is the problem. Issues like this may make you want to 'walk out', but, confronted by a grieving husband or wife, parent or child, you simply have to stay the course. They may be depending on you more than you can imagine.

> No one understands the anguish,
> No one knows the grief we share,
> As the darkness falls around us,
> No one seems to hear our prayer;
> People smother us with kindness,
> Then they walk away again:
> Their compassion flawed by blindness
> To our hurt, our fear and pain.*

Every so often, we see instances of masses of people grieving in response to the death of someone famous. You will probably remember the death of Princess Diana and the crowds throwing flowers over the cortège as it made its way out of London. For some this was evidence of a sort of mass hysteria, false grief. I have a suspicion that, in a society that still has difficulty with allowing feelings to be expressed, this event gave 'permission' for grief to be

* Andrew Pratt. Reproduced by permission of Stainer & Bell Ltd.

open and people tapped into much that was unresolved in their own lives. I have known women in their eighties who were carrying the grief of a miscarriage or abortion from 60 or more years before.

Last in this section, but by no means least, what do you believe? You cannot preach or share beliefs that are tentative unless you can admit that they are. People will notice and you will be living a lie. That will help no one.

What can I do?

One thing that you can always do is remember you are dealing with a person. Don't refer to 'the body' or 'the deceased'. This was someone's parent – think about it if it was your dad – or child – if it was your daughter, she would have a name. Remember: people, people, people.

Close behind this is the fact that your deep faith may not be shared by those with whom you are ministering. Be sensitive to what others believe, regardless of your faith or doubt. Then, keeping your integrity intact, believe what you say, say what you believe.

One of the benefits of being a minister is that of being wanted, being needed. This is never more true than at a time of death. It is an immense privilege, but it also brings great responsibility with it. It is very easy to take over.

The undertaker rang. 'Hello minister. I've booked a funeral at the crem. for Wednesday next, 11 o'clock. That all right? The hymns are . . .' I want to say, 'Hold it! Stop right there!'

The undertaker has a job to do. He or she will be organizing umpteen funerals that week, probably a number on that day. The more control the better. If everything can be tidied up, no loose ends, things will go smoothly, less stress. All of that is understandable. I'm not criticizing. Ministers can get into the same culture. We are the professionals, we know how a funeral 'should' be conducted. Much of that ethos is to ensure we have control and that nothing unpredictable happens.

Let's stop for a minute, though, and look at it from the point of view of the bereaved. I remember in a crematorium the wife of a man who had died in his early forties crying out, 'Why have you done this to me? Why?' It was a loud cry, muffled a little by sobs. Her husband had left her. Not literally, yet very literally. He had died and she had had no control over the event and little over what she was feeling. He had laid out in his will – he had been terminally ill – exactly how the funeral should proceed, so she had not even felt that she had been allowed to influence this remembrance of his life.

The point is, when someone dies, we very rarely have control over that death. Then the professionals move in and, rather than enabling us to regain a little control, they take over – 'This is the day, the time, the hymns, the prayers.' Don't get me wrong, some people need to be 'carried' through this process, but not nearly as many as you would imagine.

So, if your local undertaker tells you the hymns before you've seen the bereaved, have some understanding of his or her point of view. Nevertheless, this is not part of the undertaker's role and he or she needs to know that, when dealing with you, this is part of the ground that you will cover. Your role, my role, is to enable people to grieve, to mourn, to celebrate a life in the manner that is helpful to them and in keeping with the wishes of the person who has died, if these are known. That is not always straightforward.

I was sitting in the front room of the house. The mother had died and her son and daughter were drinking tea with me. Cutting a long story short, this is what they shared with me. Their mother's will specified that there should be *no* funeral. Now, in essence, there is nothing to prevent this, but the son and daughter, without quite putting it like this, said that they needed to both grieve and mark the significance that their mother had had in their lives. In no way, however, did they want to go against her will. She had been a strong woman whom they had respected. What could be done?

The answer was actually straightforward. The woman had asked to be cremated. The crematorium was booked for a full service – 15 minutes were allowed for committals, 20 minutes for the full service – in effect you could add five minutes to this for entering and leaving. Most crematoria work like that. On the day, the coffin was brought in with only me present. I said no words. The curtains were closed obscuring the coffin from sight. The woman's wishes had been met. The family then came in and we had a service for them. Their needs had been met.

I use this illustration as an extreme. In every situation there is going to be compromise to a greater or lesser extent, but we help people most by enabling them to do what they feel they need to do on the day of the funeral.

The practicalities

When you first hear that someone has died it is the first time you have the opportunity to let people take control. You may think that it is your place to visit immediately. Sometimes that is right, but it is best if the bereaved make the decision. So, having heard of the death, unless of course you are there, contact the bereaved when you know you have time and space to go round immediately. Sometimes this may mean leaving the call until later in the day. That is all right. When you contact them, ask when they would like you to come round, if at all. Turning up at one house in dark suit, black shirt and dog-collar having been informed of a death by the undertaker, I was greeted with 'Why are you here?' I thought it was self-evident, but the bereaved son had not asked me to come, did not want me to come and I took the funeral having learned little if anything about his father at all. My insensitivity and need to be in control, my 'knowing it all' and feeling sure that I was needed and wanted crippled my pastoral relationship before it had begun.

So, you arrange to meet. That story about the doorstep rebuttal has another lesson to teach. One of the effects of grief can be anger. The man was angry and I was the butt of that anger. Sometimes you will be, too. Remember that the anger is coming from the grief and you don't have to return it in the same way.

The first thing to do when you arrive is listen. A simple question such as, 'Tell me what happened?' can often set the ball rolling. If the bereaved person or people are incommunicative, give them space by sharing some practicalities with them. When will the funeral take place and where? What time will it be? You can say that you are just checking for your own sake. It may seem superfluous – after all, the undertaker has told you and the family the arrangements – but it is not always that simple. I remember a colleague who had gone to a crematorium for a funeral only to find that it was taking place at another venue half an hour's drive away. Luckily she was early and got to the other place just in time! Another I heard of took a lift with the undertaker to the crematorium. After the service, he got chatting with some of the congregation only to find that the undertaker had gone and he was stranded. So, I always check all the details.

Next, it's a case of asking what the people want for the funeral. Some will have a very good idea. Some will need leading. Occasionally you may become the referee, as happened when I arrived at the home of a woman who had died in her late eighties. Five adult members of the family had gathered. You could tell by occasional comments and their body language that all was not well.

The mother had been a matriarch who had held the family together, kept them in order. They were now vying for supremacy. Having checked the details and written down their names, I asked about the service. 'What do you think?' asked the eldest. This was a delicate question. Each of them was trying to get me on his or her side – this could be used against the others.

I don't suggest that you necessarily follow my example in what came next, but, in the role of referee, in this situation, it worked. 'What hymns do you want?' I asked. Each in turn gave me a hymn. They hadn't discussed this. Each hymn was different. I took down the first line of each in turn. When they'd finished, I simply said, 'Yes and what else do you want?'

Five jaws dropped simultaneously. At last, one of them said, 'Can we have five hymns?' At this I simply stated that, unless they decided which one or ones to drop, yes they could, and what else did they want? A funeral is not a time to help members of a family score points off one another.

So, the service needs to be arranged and, as far as possible, the family members should be enabled to arrange it. More often than not, it will be necessary to give them an idea of the sorts of things that are needed, not least information about the deceased, and then leave them to think, coming back in a day or two.

Sometimes one of them may want to say a word. Allow this, but be aware that he or she may not be able to and might have to drop out at the last moment, even while standing at the lectern. Your place is to enable, to support and stand in if necessary. Many people will be happy for you to do everything and even to choose hymns, but, if that is so, it is because it is their choice, a choice you've enabled, not your choice that you've thrust on them because it is more comfortable for you that way.

Music can often be a sore point. I began this chapter with the story about 'O happy day'. If that had been what they wanted, though, it would have been appropriate. What is appropriate? It is rare for me to say no to music. Usually what is chosen is either significant for the family or the deceased. The one thing I drew the line at – well, it hadn't actually been chosen, but . . . someone I knew wanted his dad to go out to a Rolling Stones track. The rest of the service had been quite conventional. The trouble was, he didn't know which Rolling Stones record. I thought back through the possibilities. 'Anything except "Sympathy for the Devil"' was my response. He chose 'Get off my cloud'. The mood fitted. On another occasion, someone wanted 'I did it my way' at the crematorium. It was in his will, 'as the curtains close, Sinatra: "now I face the final curtain"'. He had a sense of humour that man. The congregation knew that, so, again, it fitted.

If you are choosing the Bible reading(s), make sure that they are right for the person who has died and those who remain. Not all passages that speak firmly of resurrection will make sense for everyone. Again, be sensitive. A funeral is not the place to question the eternal destination of the dead, nor that of a grieving congregation!

The funeral will begin or end at a crematorium or graveside. The choice is theirs, not yours, whatever your feelings. Find out where the grave is before you walk towards it. There may be more than one prepared and you may be leading the way.

If part or all of the service is at a crematorium, check where it is. Go with the undertaker if you are at all unsure.

Before the service begins, make sure whether you need to close curtains or lower the catafalque. Often there are buttons to press for this. Sometimes an attendant listens to the service and does this for you at the right time. Make sure that he or she knows when you want this to happen.

At a church, you may be responsible for a whole raft of arrangements, from getting an organist and steward to unlocking the building. Others may do all these things for you. The important thing, again, is to know who will do what and make sure that it is done.

After a while, it is easy to get blasé. You will conduct many funerals, but each of us has only one. Remember that.

Some ministers like to leave a card or memento for the family. If you do, make sure that it is suitable. Some cards may not be. Read it carefully before you leave it.

Every death is different

Perinatal death

By this I mean death at or near to birth – the word means literally 'around birth'. Here I would include abortions, stillbirth and miscarriages as well as deaths in the first year, cot deaths and so on.

None of these can be 'swept out of the way'. For a woman to have conceived is enough for her to begin to anticipate the birth. If that birth doesn't take place, then there will be feelings that need to be dealt with.

Each situation is different. As with every death, listen to what is being said, watch how people are responding and, in turn, try to respond sensitively and sympathetically to different needs as you perceive them. Fathers have feelings too and it is worth remembering that when much attention may be focused on the mother. If there are tangible memories these are important. Parents may have an ultrasound scan or photos of a stillborn child and may have held him or her. There may well be feelings of guilt to deal with, anger or depression. In the case of a cot death, a lot of questions may be asked about what the parents did or did not do. This can be exacerbated by the presence of the police who will need to be involved in such a death.

At one level it may well seem inappropriate to baptize a dead child, but, if this is a compassionate action to take, at a parent's request, you may well want to override your theological scruples in order to offer comfort. Only you can decide. A funeral is always appropriate if this is requested and undertakers usually charge minimal expenses or even none in the case of the death of a child.

A couple I knew had been expecting twins. Both died at birth. The parents wanted a funeral, but they were well known and wanted something quiet and private, which would have been impossible in their own church. A neighbouring chapel held the service. The steward opened up, no questions asked, and came back later to lock up again. We had simple prayers and a child's hymn. Just the family members were there and they did what they needed to. Four of us – the mum, dad, the undertaker and me – witnessed the burial. It was enough.

Death of a young person

Deaths of children and young people are always hard to cope with. They should outlive us. Sometimes there has been illness, sometimes the death is sudden. It never seems 'right'. There is often a lot of anger and recrimination around. We need someone to blame. False platitudes are unhelpful – 'he's gone to be with Jesus' portrays an awful picture of Jesus. So, be careful what you say. As ever, a lot of listening is needed as the story of this child may be told and retold. You will see their toys, read their writing, be shown their pictures.

Some members of the family need this, others will recoil from it. Both attitudes are acceptable and we need to allow each, but it can cause great tension, especially between parents or with grandparents if they are present.

The funeral may well represent the child. Often the picture will be idealized. You may find it hard to believe, but it is their child, their story, their picture. A 22-year-old may be imagined as a baby or a man. Hopes and dreams will mix with memories. All are important. Parents may want to speak or be unable to. I spoke at my son's funeral and later his friends from university buried him, literally. The gravediggers let them be – they could see that this was the last thing they could do for their friend.

Accidental or sudden death

It goes without saying that this is unexpected and the response of people can be out of character.

'Can you come round, my wife's died?' said the voice on the phone. She was 40. I'd seen her Morris Dancing in the square the day before. She was fit and well. I was there inside five minutes.

Jim (that's not his actual name) opened the door. 'I hate God! You know what I mean?!' he said. The question was half shouted at me. If I hadn't said that I understood, he wouldn't have let me in. He had every right to be angry with God – his wife had just died in his arms after coming in from a day's work. He had to be angry with someone and he was trying to make sense of her death and his belief in God. He was being very biblical. There's a lot of hatred in the Bible (look at Psalm 137 for a start).

Then there are all the questions. Questions people wanted to ask them, things they wanted to say – a last 'I love you' or even 'goodbye'. Then there are the, 'Why did he go to the shops? Why didn't she look where she was going? What is God doing letting my husband have an aneurism? Why should she die doing the thing she loved?' questions. We cannot answer them, but we can listen and join in the struggle, the questioning and the emptiness. We can weep with God's people when they weep. Compassion is being beside someone with feeling – com-passion – and that's what we need to do sometimes, just be there. Then later, perhaps months later, we will go along to an inquest, still beside the person with whom God wants us to minister.

Suicide

Suicide is no longer a crime. It was once. All the same, a stigma somehow still lingers even though it shouldn't. It is a very aggressive act. It always hurts more than just the person who has died.

A woman who had been born with what today would be a slight and operable disability had lived happily with her husband, who loved her deeply for who she was. When he died, she felt that no one understood her. In many ways she was right. She tried three times to take her life before she succeeded. Her friends all asked, 'What could we have done to prevent it?' At one level the answer was 'nothing' – there was nothing anyone could have done. At another, perhaps we could have all loved her more, but we could not have brought back her husband and her love for him and his death were not our fault.

A young man, redundant after the closure of the coalmines in Lancashire, who was found by his father, died because he had no work. Lots of people have no work but don't commit suicide. For his father, though, the National Coal Board and strikebreakers brought about his son's death. All of the father's hurt came pouring out for a lost life and purpose, his son's and his own.

As we minister, we listen and reflect and offer honest compassion to those who grieve as they mourn, but also suffer from the anger that cannot be vented on the one who has died.

Terminal illness

However long you've waited, the death is still always sudden.

In some ways, terminal illness can enable those who are watching and those who are dying to prepare for the inevitable. It is true that, as people watch someone losing physical strength, they can begin to mourn. I mourned not being able to play football with my father again as he succumbed to multiple sclerosis and lung cancer long before he died.

For some, loss of personality as dementia sets in means that they are no longer recognized by the one they love. Misdiagnoses can be tantalizingly painful as we prepare for one thing, only to be told that the person is dying from something completely different.

Then, when the death comes, we have had so much time to ask what might have been, what we might have done to make things different, we question the quality of care and the depth of love that we have offered. We question the extent of the suffering and whether or how it could have been ameliorated. We grieve.

The 'grief process'

Friend of the world, bright shining sun!
Reeling and dancing, life begun;
living and learning, climbing high,
soaring on wings as if to fly.

Autumn is coming to the trees,
colour is drained from falling leaves;
darkness is covering all the earth,
his dance goes on, it finds new birth.*

There is plenty of literature on what has come to be known as the 'grief process'. I have not mentioned it until now because I believe that it needs to be treated with care.

As this chapter has progressed, I have shared a number of stories of people who have died and those who have grieved for them. What becomes clear as we consider them is that the responses of people vary and we must add to this that they vary over time. That having been said, many people have similar responses, so an analysis of grief responses makes sense. The idea of a 'process' is less helpful, though, as not all people pass through the different stages in a predictable sequence.

In outline, the following feelings are often associated with grief.

- Initially there can be a numbness or denial – 'This can't be possible!' For some, this is can become a permanent way of coping. The person goes on as though nothing has changed.
- People yearn for the person who has died to be there and do things to make their reality continue – laying an extra place at the table, for instance. A room can become a shrine.

- There can be bargaining – 'If I do this, then it won't be true.'
- There is often a sense of guilt – 'If I'd done X, he or she wouldn't have died.'
- Tears and sadness, which can be part of or a precursor to depression, are common. Sleeplessness, physical heaviness, changed eating patterns and so on can all be symptomatic of this.
- Anger is a common emotion, whether it is directed at the person who has died, another member of the family, the hospital or a doctor or God – someone is to blame.
- A mix of guilt and anger can sometimes result in suicidal tendencies or self-harm.

Ultimately, the bereaved person may well move to a point of accepting the death and begin to live life in this new reality.

The important thing to remember when counselling people who have been bereaved is that each person may exhibit some or all of the above reactions. Each response may come or go more than once during the period of bereavement. It is unhelpful to talk about 'getting over' a death. It is more a case of coming to terms with a new reality. At one time it was fashionable to 'enable' people through this process. For some, that may still be helpful, but everyone is different and it does not help to try to make someone respond 'to help them along'.

For Christian ministers, there is an additional warning. We believe in resurrection, but an overemphasis on this element of faith can elicit a negative response from someone who is unable to feel that this is a reality. Equally, the doctrine of resurrection can be used by people as a way of denying the reality of what has happened. Also, 'he has been raised' does not always equate helpfully with what our senses tell us, which is that he, or his mortal remains, have actually just been buried deep in the ground.

'God, I hate you!'
Screams the anger
Of my stone cold grief;
God, I need you
In this anguished,
Taunting misbelief.

God, I love you
In my anger,
Dispossessed by grief;
Love me even
Though I hate you;
Hold me, show me peace.*

---

* Andrew Pratt. Reproduced by permission of Stainer & Bell Ltd.

Afterwards

Some people may want to see you after the funeral. If so, offer them a visit. Go if they want you to, but don't take offence if they don't. You will remind them of the death no matter what you do.

Keep a record of the dates of deaths and funerals and be aware of the anniversaries. Some people who have been bereaved may not remember the date, but that way you will be sensitive to the fact for those who do. This practice may also help you to pick up on responses they make many months on when the grief comes back to the surface, sometimes for no apparent reason.

Summary

1. You are working with people, not just faceless bodies.
2. Know what you believe, but listen to what others believe.
3. Do not force your faith on others.
4. Be prepared.
5. Enable others to have as much control in relation to the death as you can, arranging details, planning the funeral and so on.
6. Go on caring.

Looking ahead

- Listen to anyone with experience who may give you insight or advice – other ministers, undertakers, counsellors.
- Evaluate what you hear as not all of it may help you.
- Take a counselling course.

Chapter 9
Meetings – yes, meetings!

A group of adolescents met in the manse every Monday evening. Looking back now, they were no different from any other normal teenagers, but they seemed formidable. Having had a teenage son, I say with affection that they ranged from Einstein to orang-utan!

From time to time, I invited visitors to come and talk with them. On one occasion, a swashbuckling ex-military chap came, thinking that he'd impress them with his exploits. He limped away from the experience. At times, they had me at my wits' end even though I had taught youngsters of this age. The trouble in their case was that the usual rules and regulations didn't exist. This was altogether freer.

One Sunday evening, I'd invited someone from Social Services who had been involved in childcare. She was a diminutive woman with a strong character. The youngsters were in the lounge, sitting and lying around the room in ways that I sometimes think are only possible at that age. She came in and quietly, without saying a word, sat on the floor at a point in the room where she could see them all, but was also physically on a lower level than all of them. She sat and she waited. You could have heard a pin drop. She had totally disarmed them. They were a little ill at ease.

Everyone else had tried to dominate them. Her approach was different and they just did not know how to react. Needless to say, the evening went well and at the end of it they were chatting away with her as if she was a friend. She still had the upper hand, though.

I tell this story because there is far more to handling meetings of all kinds well than just the agenda. Meetings are a necessary part of church life, not just an irritation. Without meetings of one form or another there would be no intercommunication between people, no learning, no growth. Meetings are the essence of a social organization. We need to know how to handle them well in order to work effectively with one another in God's service. Without this skill, we run the risk of wasting our own time and that of other people, too.

Where shall I sit?

Where we sit in a room, how the room is laid out, the type of seating – all these things can have an effect on the way a meeting goes. Also, different meetings will require, ideally, different settings.

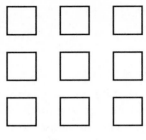

Figure 1

In Figure 1, the blocks represent chairs in a room. As people come in, the last chair to be filled is likely to be the middle one, the first that furthest from the door. There are reasons for this and they are important. They are the same reasons that lead people to sit at the back of the church rather than in the front seats.

Imagine you are an impala going to a waterhole. You have every sense alert, aware of possible predators that might attack and eat you. Hard-wired into our psyche is that animal need for protection, so someone going into an empty restaurant, given the choice, will normally take a seat by the wall where they can see the door. It's all down to animal instinct and the need for self-preservation. In a church the 'predator' is the preacher! So, you sit as far away as possible!

Knowing this can help us to understand why some rooms make us, and others, feel vulnerable. It also allows us to structure the environment we have to the best advantage for the particular purpose we have in mind. Here are some suggestions.

An informal discussion meeting is best enabled by a seating plan that ensures no one dominates, not even the 'leader'. You might like to try this some time. Put a group of chairs in a circle – enough for the intended number of people coming to the meeting. Ensure that all the chairs are the same. Let people arrive at the meeting and then join them in whatever chair is available – having let them all sit first.

At this point, there is no obvious leader. As you join, there will probably be an expectation that you will lead. Sit and wait. See how long you can sustain this. Eventually someone will ask you what they should be doing. The chairs have evened out the people in one sense – no one is in a dominant situation – but then anticipated roles and personalities come into play. It is difficult to achieve complete equality, however hard you try.

Designating a leader other than yourself can, however, change the focus. Such a layout is useful for Bible study or even a more formal discussion meeting where you want to give as many people as possible a voice.

If you want to neutralize your own dominance, you could try sitting outside the circle – the equivalent of the Social Services lady sitting on the floor with the teenagers, as in our earlier story – or stay out of the meeting altogether.

Many ministers would find these last options difficult. However much we talk of 'collaborative leadership' and 'enabling the laity', we each have a wish to dominate, to control. Again, the reason is psychological. The more control we have, the more certain we can be of the outcome of a situation. The more certain we are, the less likely it is that we will to be surprised or unsettled. It all comes back to our own confidence.

Let us assume for a moment that the congregation you are minister of wants to discuss the possibility of extending the church building – just a matter of should we or shouldn't we? Do you need to influence the decision? You may want to – if they don't go ahead, your pet project cannot get off the ground. Step back for moment, here. Realistically, the members of the congregation were probably there before you arrived as minister and they will be there after you've left. They will reap the benefits and shoulder the burden of any decision that is made. So, they need to make that decision aside from any agenda you may have. Let them get on with it.

Well, yes, but what role do you have? Part of the role is having enough personal security to let go and let them get on with it. Your role is likely to be advisory and prophetic, bearing in mind that what you say, because of your role, will probably have an undue influence on some people – 'the Minister said . . .'. What do I mean by advisory or prophetic? You are, first and foremost, the minister. You have the task of enabling people to discern God's will. That can mean pointing them to Scripture or making them pause for prayer. Sometimes you will need to say that a particular expenditure is plain wrong or the way of funding it is unacceptable for a church, but be careful that you do not dress up your own prejudice or bias as being 'God's will'. At other times, you will need to make people decide for themselves – not because you do not care, but because it is genuinely their responsibility. As an adviser, you will sometimes need to know the legal and financial consequences of actions so that you can guide not only the decision-making process but also the way in which decisions are later implemented. On occasion, the field of decision may need to be limited because of what is legally possible in terms of, say, a lease or covenant.

Once the discussion has taken place, you may need a more formal meeting structure. This might be enabled in the same meeting where you now formally 'take the chair'. In this role, opinions are balanced and arguments heard. Often, the distinction between one sort of meeting outcome and another is blurred and you need to operate subtly to enable different agendas to be met. This is true in a Bible study as much as a business meeting.

I once led a Bible study with some ten people of widely differing theological perspectives. One was plainly fundamentalist, another liberal and radical and the others in between. There are two ways to approach such a meeting. One is to give a firm lead – your opinion is to dominate. Sometimes there will be a cultural expectation that this is what you will do, even should do. Another is to engender respect and enable discussion. Very early on, this particular group, on my suggestion, accepted the latter way. They set down some ground rules:

- everyone should be allowed to speak without interruption
- while there could be debate and even argument, each had to respect the others' right to hold a different point of view.

The result was that the debate, argument and discussion were often vigorous, yet the meetings always ended amicably and with prayer and blessing. Friendships were forged and deepened. People learned and grew. Just occasionally, my role was that of referee, reminding them of the ground rules that they had accepted. I could lead with integrity, knowing that my own views were held to be equally as valid as those of everyone else. Of course, if you are absolutely sure of the rightness of your own interpretation of Scripture, this may be anathema, but, time and again, I have marvelled at how people grow in love, fellowship and understanding when this sort of interchange is enabled.

In a business meeting, the same sense of balance is often needed. As chair of a meeting, your role is to enable discussion but also to lead people towards making appropriate decisions. The seating layout can signify your role, though be conscious of how this can affect people's ability to share and indicate your dominance.

The more focused the seating plan, the more separate your chair, the less open will be discussion and the greater will be the influence of your lead. (See Figure 2, where C indicates the chair.

Ultimately there will be times when you need to show authority for the right reasons – not because of your insecurity, but out of the necessity to give a strong lead.

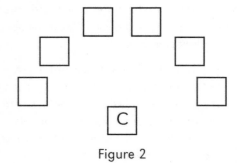

Figure 2

Imagine an old church in which people wish to remove the pews and replace them with chairs. The church happens to be a listed building. Within the church are groups with very different views on the way forward. One group simply want to explore the possibility of removing the pews at the earliest opportunity. Another group wish to retain the pews at all costs. Between are some people who want to explore the option, but also look at the possibility of retaining an historic building while making more use of other premises owned by the church.

Usually in these situations each group will assume that they know what the other groups want and why. They have probably never talked to each other. So, you enable a meeting in the round just to allow discussion. At the end of the meeting, they all have a better idea of what the others think. They also become aware that there are people who have been quiet who also have opinions and conclude that the feelings of the whole church need to be canvassed. So, a questionnaire is organized and the results collated. The end point is that the majority do not want to change the church, but do want to look at how the rest of the premises are used. You become aware that, at the meeting to look at the way ahead, some members of the church are going to press for removal of the pews anyway. They do not accept the results of the questionnaire. You are sure that these results should be accepted and need to enable the church to find a way forward.

In this situation, you need to see everyone, they need to see you and it might be best if they have little direct eye contact with each other. This gives you control. You affirm the results of the questionnaire, allow for the challenge and then reaffirm the result. From this point onwards, the church needs to go forward with the reality of the democratic voice that has been heard. You may wish to take things forward here or convene another meeting. Again, the layout of the meeting has enabled the appropriate atmosphere to be created for what needed to be done.

Preparing for a meeting

A meeting of a number of churches was scheduled for 7.30 p.m. one evening. At 7.25 p.m., a steward turned up with no key. Three minutes later, the steward who did have the key arrived. By the time the tables and chairs were arranged, the meeting got underway at 7.45 p.m. People were not in a good mood and went away at 9.30 p.m. in a worse one.

A neighbouring church had a similar meeting arranged. At 7 p.m., the doors were opened. A cup of tea was handed to each person as they arrived. Some had come straight from work, so the tea was especially welcome. The meeting began at 7.30 p.m. as scheduled, but didn't end until 10 p.m. Folk hung around chatting and the doors of the church were finally locked at 10.30 p.m. The general feeling was that it had been a good meeting.

Both these scenarios are real. I dare not divulge the names of the churches! Each congregation just did it their way. As a church leader, you cannot guarantee that members of a church will prepare in the way you would wish until you have set things in motion and established the procedures that you need or want. Do not assume that things will happen in a right or helpful way. Ask how they get ready for a meeting, who is responsible for opening and closing the church, laying it out and providing refreshments, if they are needed.

> Here we meet to seek God's purpose,
> catch a glimpse of given grace,
> find a way to mirror goodness
> in this present time and place.
>
> Walk with love, the future beckons,
> now we need to deepen trust,
> recognize a common purpose,
> mutual care, less cut and thrust.
>
> Best of all, our God is with us
> as we frame each concrete scheme,
> as we answer human questions,
> as we try to live a dream.*

Within the meeting itself, people need to know who is expected to do what. Does the secretary book the room or someone else? Make sure that every eventuality you can envisage is covered until you know the system and have people on whom you can rely to enable things to happen smoothly.

Meetings that need to be minuted should have a secretary who can take those minutes.

One time, the secretary of a church council meeting took what he regarded to be accurate minutes. At the following meeting, the minutes were aggressively challenged. At the next meeting, the secretary brought a voice recorder, put it in a prominent position so everyone could see it and told them why it was there. At the following church council meeting, the members were presented with full verbatim minutes. This was not at all ideal, but did make a point!

You may need to train a secretary who is taking the minutes and then be willing to defend them.

Minutes should contain enough information for those looking back to understand why a particular decision was made, over and against another

---

* Andrew Pratt. Reproduced by permission of Stainer & Bell Ltd.

possibility. Individuals may sometimes need to be identified. It should be clear who is to take action relating to the minutes.

In the case of a meeting where people are making legal decisions, effectively acting as trustees, the names and addresses of all those attending should be recorded in the minute book, even if these are not distributed with the minutes.

Minutes should rarely, if ever, be read out by the secretary at the meeting. Instead, they should be distributed as soon as possible after the meeting to allow people to be reminded of decisions they made and actions they are expected to take. Within the minutes, it is helpful to highlight these points.

Prior to distribution, the chair should see the minutes to allow for any corrections or clarification to be made. You can then support the secretary in the event of a dispute.

Today, for many people, all of this can be done by e-mail, speeding the process up and saving on paper and postage. Prior to the next meeting, the chair should meet or communicate with the secretary and any other necessary officers to determine matters arising from the previous minutes, progress that has been made on matters put in hand, matters to report and items to include in the next agenda. We have now gone full circle, returning to the reminder being given to members of the next meeting.

All that has been said here relates to a formal church meeting, but could usefully be adapted for a variety of meetings of a more informal nature.

Chairing a meeting

Within a meeting, the chair has an enabling role. Listening skills are essential for this and meticulous preparation will enable the flow of the meeting.

A scientist who had been studying the behaviour of insect swarms decided to apply something of what he had learned to staff meetings. He tried to go into meetings with an open mind, not to lead, and allow people to work out for themselves possible solutions to problems. He used sealed ballots for decisions. Things seemed to move more smoothly and work out more effectively than before.

It should be clear from what you have read in this chapter so far that different meetings work with different criteria, using different strategies. It is the role of the chair, with knowledge of the agenda, to decide which way forward is best for a particular meeting or a particular phase of a meeting.

I remember a minster chairing a church council, who, when he had had enough of a topic, would move people on regardless of what point the discussion had reached. In many meetings, it is essential to make decisions and record who is responsible for actioning them. Again, it is the responsibility of the chair to work out not only what decisions need to be made but also how they can be made and then ensure that they are acted on. That does not mean taking on all the work yourself, but ensuring that someone knows what to do and that they are committed to doing it.

In practice, this may mean deciding, for instance, that a task needs to be done (decision 1), it needs to be costed (decision 2) and who will do the costing (decision 3). Put like this, it all seems logical, but, without the guidance of the chair, people will sometimes waste time arguing about who is going to do something or how it will be paid for before the group has even decided whether or not the action should be taken.

Often, there will need to be a system in place to ensure that actions have actually been taken, a channel for feedback, perhaps before the next gathering.

Listening is critical because some people may have something useful to offer, but be afraid to say it. The chair should enable contributions to be made safely, without ridicule. Sometimes one person will be talking a lot, but saying little. He or she will need to be politely, but effectively, constrained. A good ploy may be to ask another member of the group to reflect on what has been said. Occasionally, the chair becomes a referee, enabling disparate opinions to be safely shared.

Whose meeting is it anyway?

A couple of months before arriving at a new appointment, I received a letter. It told me about someone in the church in a level of detail and tone that would have been libellous if it had become public. As I opened the letter, it immediately became apparent what its nature was. I sealed it up again and sent it back, saying that I neither needed nor wanted to know the information that it contained.

When I was a teacher, even though I tried, I couldn't avoid hearing what other teachers thought about the pupils, good or bad. I tried not to be influenced, but it wasn't easy. Similarly, you will hear all manner of things about people in your church – make your own judgments, trying not to be influenced. Another person's negative comments can often say more about them than the person they are criticizing.

Meetings bring all those people together, with all their prejudices, scars and misapprehensions. However much you may want to hold to a theology of the body of Christ where you are on a par with them all, part of your role is to enable them to be that body together. Some will think that they own a meeting. Others will always have been made to think that they have nothing valuable to offer. The meeting is a microcosm of the world and can be just as cruel. Sometimes you will need to encourage, at others defend, at still other times to restrain. You must, nevertheless, be evenhanded.

To be able to achieve this will sometimes require that you maintain a necessary distance from those with whom you minister. This is not fashionable, but it is true. You have been set apart, in ordination or whatever process your congregation or denomination chooses to use to recognize your ministry, for a role in the Church. Your task is not always easy, yet the theological understanding that encompasses it all is the infinite value of each individual and the corporate nature of the Church. Added to that is your own calling and the fact that this is God's work in which you have been called to be instrumental.

So now I come to finding an answer to the question that began this section. Each meeting in a church belongs to the people of that church under God – it just may not always look like that!

Remember:

You need not raise your eyes up to the mountains,
or travel to a rich and royal seat,
amid this crowd God's love can spring in fountains;
the God you seek is kneeling at your feet.

Summary
1.   Meetings involve people.
2.   Know the people with whom you are working.
3.   Be prepared.
4.   Decide what the purpose of the meeting is.
5.   Decide the best setting and layout for the meeting.
6.   Enable others to participate, but give a lead when it is necessary.

Looking ahead
*   Find someone you can trust to give constructive feedback on how you handle meetings.
*   Do not be afraid to read secular books and papers on management.

Chapter 10
Managing change

Change is difficult to cope with, but inevitable. One task facing those who minister in the Church is that of enabling change to take place. Sometimes it is forced change that cannot be predicted or prepared for. Sometimes it is a change that has been chosen.

When there is choice involved, there are certain basic principles that it is worth considering.

1. Is the change necessary?
    Many changes take place for the sake of change. This question ought to be asked and answered seriously.

2. How soon does it need to happen?
    If the change is necessary, this is the next question to ask. Changes are often rushed through too quickly. Time taken can be time well used in assessing priorities and making right choices.

3. How soon would you like it to happen?
    The answer to this should be realistic. You may want to do something immediately, but it is important to assess the consequences of change.

4. How soon would other key people like it to happen?
    Others may not have the same expectations regarding the timetable for the change as you.

5. What conflicts do you anticipate?
    Trying to guess areas of conflict is not easy, but, if you know where you are likely to run into opposition, it is sometimes possible to at least minimize it.

6. What avoidance action ought you to take?
    Some actions can enable you to avoid problems that you have foreseen.

7. What is the timetable for the change?
    Set a timetable so that, within it, you can plan the change. In this way it will not just happen randomly.

8. How will people be informed and carried along with the process?
    The timetable should enable you to prepare people for change before it occurs and then take them along with you through the process.

9. Which key people need to be involved and at what level?
    Change will often involve people other than yourself. Try to determine who they should be and when they should be involved. Some people may need more involvement than others because of their role.

10. What is the process?
    As far as you can, work out what the stages in the process are that will enable you to achieve the aim.

To demonstrate how these principles work out in practice, let me share two real scenarios with you. The first involved planned, considered change. The second was change in response to a crisis.

Let's get together!

Some denominations organize their congregations in groups that are, to a greater or lesser extent, independent of each other. Methodism has groupings called circuits, which have a number of congregations with, usually, a team of ordained ministers and lay people sharing the work of the Church. The team is overseen by a Superintendent. Circuits are grouped in Districts under the care of a Chair of District.

In this particular instance, two circuits were going to come together. One had ten congregations with four ordained ministers, the other five with, unusually, one ordained minister. The answer to question 1 was a 'yes' because it was not regarded as good practice to have one ordained minister working solo.

The matter of timing raised by questions 2 and 3 was more complicated. The change had to fit in with other constraints, including the timings of the ministers' appointments and the running of the Church year from an administrative point of view. Clearly the changes needed to be made as soon as possible – that is often the case – but how soon was it going to be possible to do so?

The views of other people varied. Some saw no point in making the change at all. Change is always threatening to some people, even if the status quo is unsatisfactory. Remember, the complaint of the people of Israel in the wilderness, that they would rather be back in slavery in Egypt? The feelings of these people still had to be taken into account and time was required to enable them to join the journey. Other people would have been happy for the change to have been made within months, at the next Methodist year end.

As is often the case, the possible conflicts were self-evident. The structuring of the timetable was arranged, in part, to mitigate these conflicts.

Let us jump to question 9. In the first instance, a meeting was called of the two Superintendent Ministers, the Chair of District and senior lay officers of each circuit. The need for the change was discussed and agreed. Concerns were expressed about the larger circuit 'taking over' the smaller one. Thus, communication had to take place not only across the circuits but also to the grass roots of each congregation.

A second meeting was planned and, at that stage, there was no definite projected end point for the process. Representatives of each congregation were called to the meeting. The proposal of amalgamation was put before them and, in groups, they were asked to look at the pros and cons of the projected changes. The responses of the groups were collated on a flipchart. The meeting ended with refreshments to enable informal conversation. Another meeting of the same constituents was convened a month later.

In the meantime, the Superintendents, Chair and circuit officers met again. They looked over the responses of the groups. Where questions of fact needed to be answered, these were explored and answers provided to the next meeting. At the end of the next meeting, a decision was made by the whole group as to whether or not it was feasible and appropriate to proceed.

At this point, the decision was in the affirmative, but note that only certain specific people had been involved in the process so far. The decision was still very much 'in principle'. The next step was for each circuit to hold a meeting at which its own congregations were fully represented to look at the prospect of proceeding further. These meetings took place, but it was felt that the consequences needed to be made known to each constituent congregation. Thus, a 'roadshow' was prepared that went to each congregation in turn to offer information and answer questions. Only then was a formal decision made by each circuit to move towards amalgamation.

It was then necessary to work out how the circuits would be administered, who would be appointed as Superintendent, how the pastoral care of the congregations would be divided and what timescale all this could be achieved in. It was then necessary to make projections about the future staffing of the new circuit post amalgamation in order that the service of union that marked the coming together was not seen as an end in itself. In all, the process took some three years.

Did it work? Well, the circuits did amalgamate. When churches or circuits join, there is usually some loss of disaffected members. We knew what the membership of the two circuits was prior to amalgamation. We also knew what the rate of decline in membership over the whole district was for the two years prior to amalgamation and for the two years afterwards. The decline in membership of the uniting circuits afterwards was less steep than it was before it, so, in a numerical sense, the change had been successful. The effects of the changes on the ground, however, were more difficult to assess, but the goal of ensuring that an ordained minister was no longer working in isolation had been met.

It all came tumbling down!

The second scenario I want to share with you relates to a crisis. Every so often, it is wise for church buildings to be inspected by a qualified architect or surveyor. On one such occasion, the architect visiting this particular church asked that a building engineer be employed to give a second opinion. On visiting the building, the engineer informed me verbally that the building was unsafe and the roof was liable to collapse. This was not only a danger to those inside the building, but, if the roof did collapse, it would probably push the walls outwards and anyone standing near them could be hurt.

One of the underlying principles of risk management is that, from the point at which you are notified of a risk, you become liable for the consequences of that risk. Put simply, now I had been told of the danger, if the roof was to collapse and someone was hurt or some property was damaged and I had taken no steps to mitigate this, I would bear some liability in law.

In this instance, the change that needed to be made following this news was necessary and it had to be made immediately. I notified a member of the church and, in conversation, he expressed the feeling that to close the church and prevent people from parking their cars near it would be an over-reaction. The conflict that accompanies change was already being demonstrated and, in this instance, there was no time to enlist other support.

A simple statement relating to my own liability and the fact that our insurance would be invalidated if we did nothing needed to be made there and then. The congregation met in another part of the building, which was safe, on the following Sunday. They were told what had happened and that a meeting was urgently needed to address the situation.

In the meantime, the structural engineer was employed to make the building 'safe'. This action incurred a cost, which would be ongoing in terms of hiring supporting scaffolding. The church did not have unlimited funds, so needed to act quickly.

The necessary meeting was convened. It was an open meeting for anyone who wished to attend and not limited only to members. The discussion was open and it became clear that there were at least five distinct solutions to the problem. These ranged from putting the roof back as it had been originally to closing the church and joining with a congregation of another denomination with which they had good relations, this being just 100 metres away. A meeting was convened for one week's time and a representative of each scheme agreed to present their ideas to this meeting for consideration.

The pressure was on to move swiftly, but it was also important to take these disparate factions along together. The Church Secretary ensured that everyone was informed at every stage and notes of meetings were posted regularly in the room where the congregation was now meeting Sunday by Sunday.

At the next meeting, each representative was allowed to speak for ten minutes without interruption to put a case. Five minutes were allowed for questions. There was a brief amount of time given to clarifying points where this was needed, followed by a short time spent in prayer. Everyone was conscious of the need to move to a workable conclusion.

Each scheme was voted on in turn by a secret ballot. The votes were counted and recorded. After the voting, the option with the fewest votes was excluded and everyone voted again. The process continued until two options were left and then a final vote was taken.

In this way the decision was made that the roof would be replaced, but in a redesigned form to prevent a further collapse. The hope was expressed that all would work together to this end and the existence of the congregation as a part of the body of Christ was more important than any individual's hope for the future of the church.

The transition was not easy. Building works of this scale involve raising money, employment of professionals and a lot of hard work. The church was ultimately reopened and, although some people felt that the wrong decision had been made, they were still there to express their feelings!

Change goes on

You may never have to manage changes like those outlined above, but they serve to illustrate, I hope, the application of the principles that I outlined at the beginning of this chapter. Hopefully you can use these to make changes that you do have to manage less damaging and more effective.

Summary

1. Use the material in this section to ask questions about proposed changes.
2. Plan changes carefully even when they need to be made swifly.
3. Be willing to delegate tasks and get help from other people, professionally if necessary.

Looking ahead

- Try to develop the patience to wait for changes that are worthwhile.
- Try to develop the courage to initiate change swiftly but sympathetically when this is necessary.

Chapter 11
Can I help you?

Having looked at a variety of areas in which ministers, lay or ordained, meet with people and enable them to relate to each other, respond to life changes and death or enter into the body of the Church, it seems sensible to now draw together some general principles of pastoral care.

Jesus was once confronted by a group of angry people. They had stones in their hands and were bent on killing a woman. The law was on their side or so it seemed. Look up the story in John 8.1–11. The people bring their case to Jesus. The woman is an adulterer. The law indicates that the punishment for this is death by stoning. All quite straightforward. Notice how Jesus responds. He 'bent down and wrote with his finger on the ground' (verse 6). I imagine a long silence, no eye contact, the people waiting, wondering what he was going to say. Then come those famous words: 'Let anyone among you who is without sin be the first to throw a stone at her' (verse 7). Jesus looks back at the ground. Again, silence. No condemnation of the people in the crowd, simply a suggestion. Then they are left to think and, one by one, the accusers disperse.

I tell that story because it encapsulates some important lessons we can adopt in relation to our counselling of others. Jesus is presented with a serious conflict situation. He avoids eye contact as it would heighten the tension. He does not condemn the woman's accusers but, rather, suggests that they think about themselves. That is enough. It is as though he held up a mirror and said, 'Take a look at yourselves.'

There are a number of implied questions here, too. Why is the woman being accused? What is the motivation of the accusers? What is the status of the woman?

When we meet with people who need our pastoral care or counselling, often we find ourselves in similar, if less heightened, situations.

He left me

She told a story of a husband who 'had left her'. The words are in quotes because things are rarely ever as they appear. If her story is taken at face value, she is to be pitied and needs sympathy. That may be so. We will only find out if we begin by listening, listening, listening.

We signal our interest in what a person has to say by making eye contact and occasionally seeking clarification, saying, 'You mean this?' or 'Was it like that?' No judgment is offered. There is no threat. You need to hear her story as she (it could be he) is relating it.

Only when you have listened to all there is to be said do you add anything to that story. Even then, this might be by means of a question. This approach mirrors Jesus' words to the crowd. You might say, 'Why did he leave?' No judgment still, just helping thoughts to be engaged. Such a question enables her to continue. Perhaps she would say something like 'He went off with someone else'. Then ask another question – 'Why do you think he did that?'

Notice how in this scenario the minister is simply enabling the other person to think and express thoughts in words. The words are not given. There is sometimes silence, waiting. Anyone who has been a volunteer for Samaritans, answering the telephone, will tell you that silences can sometimes last many, many minutes. In that quiet, thoughts are being confronted, ideas being addressed. If you interject, the process will be stopped or redirected. Immense patience is needed in this process. Then, when the words eventually come, they are real, reflecting real feelings. Another brief question can follow – 'How do you feel about that?'

In this example, there is an underlying supposition that, when a relationship breaks down, it is rarely one-sided. If one person walks out, what has the other person done to instigate this? Relationships are rarely simple.

There is a further lesson to be learned from Jesus and the adulterer. When her accusers have gone, he asks who condemns her. For the charge to have been brought, she was undoubtedly guilty. All the accusers have gone. Neither does Jesus condemn her. That is critical – she is human and, whatever her past, God's grace and the value placed on each individual is underlined by the need for her to move forward renewed. If the shadow of condemnation continues to rest on her, she is unlikely to change. If there is no condemnation, she might just be able to live out what Jesus hopes for her when he says, 'Go your way, and from now on do not sin again' (verse 11).

Mirror, mirror . . .

Where does this put us as ministers?

In this sort of situation, we are trying to help someone to speak the words of a feeling too dangerous to be expressed. That may be a feeling of real hatred or self-loathing, perhaps, or something apparently lesser, but, for that person, just as difficult to admit to and, therefore, recognize. It could bring her face to face with her own responsibility for her feelings and the situation in which she finds herself, then on to find its root and then on to address it.

The minister, counselling her, acts like a mirror, reflecting back to her what she is saying, sometimes rephrasing what has been said, sometimes asking questions that lead the conversation forward. We are helping people to articulate their thoughts and feelings.

This form of counselling is non-directive and some may resist it. It is easier to offer solutions, to make suggestions. You walk away from the situation feeling that you have solved the problem. Sometimes that will be so, but more often you will have helped someone to avoid addressing an issue that will crop up again later and still need to be worked through. Sometimes your interjection will have answered the person's first question, but what is most important may still be beneath the surface. It will stay there until the person has confidence in you. Only after an hour of conversation, or more, will the person get to what is really bothering him or her.

You have to decide how directive you need to be, but remember that you are seeking the best for the people with whom you are ministering, not your own comfort or apparent success. You are not trying to come out of this just feeling good.

When two or three . . .

So far, I have assumed that you are meeting with a single person. Especially where relationships are involved, you may be working with more than one. What if the person we have been sharing with has his or her partner there? The unwillingness of other authorities to get involved in domestic disputes indicates something of the minefield into which we are walking.

When two or more people are involved, the minister's role may become a little like that of a referee. If this is going to be constructive, though, it is not simply a matter of keeping warring parties apart – they need to be enabled to hear each other. To continue the analogy of the mirror, it is as though you help each individual to see him- or herself but also from the other person's point of view.

Let us begin with a simple rule of thumb. Make sure that each person has the opportunity to speak without interruption. When they have finished, asking a question such as, 'What do you think she was saying to you?' can clarify whether or not the other party really was listening and, more importantly, hearing what was being said. Sometimes it may be necessary to rephrase a comment until both parties agree with the meaning. You are then acting like a translator, enabling communication.

What next?

At the end of a conversation with an individual or a dialogue between two or more people, it is important to agree what happens next. It may not be what you would want in a situation, but it ought to be something to which all those involved are committed. There may be a need for time to think, to take on board all that has been said or thought. Practical actions may need to be taken. Another meeting could be arranged.

> Dynamic God, the essence of our being,
> foundation of the 'is' and 'is to be',
> the origin of all that has been given,
> our means of living, teach us to be free.
>
> Prophetic God, disturb us in our comfort,
> then challenge our indifference, face to face.
> Bring home the fact that mercy without justice,
> or justice without mercy cripples grace.
>
> Dynamic voice, ring out through all creation,
> then speak to individuals with your care,
> that held within a cosmic contradiction
> of judgment, heaven, hell, your love is there.

Respect

In all of this, be aware of what the appropriate boundaries are between you and those you visit or meet with. It is all too easy to manipulate people who are vulnerable or take advantage of those who trust you. Your own congregation or denomination may well have guidelines on what is appropriate behaviour for a minister.

In addition, we need to be aware of issues of child protection and the protection of vulnerable adults. If you become aware of instances of alleged abuse, there is no option but to involve the appropriate authorities – initially the police. Gone are the days when a minister might try to deal with such issues and 'smooth things over'.

Be careful not to collude with abuse by siding with one person or another. If someone has 'left home', for instance, there may be a good reason for that. To not go back may be in their best interests.

From your own point of view, ensure that, as far as is possible, you never put yourself in a position where it can be alleged that you behaved inappropriately. This will mean that children and vulnerable adults are never in your sole care or company.

A final, but very important, point – do not get out of your depth. You are not the only source of counselling on the planet. You may need to refer people, to other agencies or sources of support. This is not a sign of failure, but an indication of wisdom.

Summary
1. Listen, listen, listen.
2. Your job is not primarily to judge but care.
3. Help others to hear their own feelings.
4. Help people to listen to and understand one another.

Looking ahead
- Enhance your listening skills.
- Go on a counselling course.

Chapter 12
Using your time

It is easy in ministry to feel as though you are at everybody's beck and call. A wise retired minister once said to me when I was having a moan about this, 'No you're not, you are available.' There is world of difference. To be at everybody's beck and call means that, when someone rings, you go; if someone asks you to lead a meeting, you lead it – that your time is never your own. I will be unpopular with some people for what I am going to say in this chapter, but I believe that it needs to be said.

Those of us who enter ministry are usually highly motivated and want to please. We have in mind Jesus' words: 'Jesus said to them, "My food is to do the will of him who sent me and to complete his work"' (John 4.34). The logic is, 'food is needed to live, therefore doing God's will is to live, therefore, when someone calls, I jump'. We forget in this that Jesus spent 40 days and nights in the wilderness, away from people, before he ever began his ministry and at other times sought solitude. With Martha, Mary and Lazarus, he seems to have had a bolthole to 'get away from it all'.

So, as they say, 'If I wanted to go there, I wouldn't begin from here!' The 'there' is ministry and we need to begin from a premise other than a food one. I speak as someone who has worked in different environments as well as full-time ordained ministry. Again, what I have to say may not be well received. Ministry, in my experience – and I don't just mean that of the ivory tower of college tutors – is one of the most privileged environments in which to work that I know of.

Expectations

Those who minister on a full-time basis, if they have no conscience, can get away with doing very little. We are expected to conduct a certain number of services on a Sunday and perhaps during the week. There is an expectation that we will visit people at times of crisis, though not all ministers do. We have an obligation within our Church's structures to be present at certain meetings, but not nearly as many as most ministers make out! These are the things that we have to do.

A lot of other things can crowd in on us. We can be asked to go to this meeting, that fellowship, lead this group or serve on that committee. Our predecessor may have done all of these things and more. Our predecessor may be recuperating after a breakdown!

So, what do we do? I am not counselling you to be lazy – far from it. Rather, I am counselling you to be responsible to the command to 'love ourselves' that others might be loved.

Where do we begin?

In the beginning . . .

'In the beginning. . . the earth was a formless void' (Genesis 1.1–2). When you begin a new appointment, save for the arrangements your predecessor has made for you, you are in charge of your diary and it will be without form and largely void or ought to be. This is one of the privileges of ministry. Beyond the expectations and obligations listed above, your time is your own to order as you please. Well, not quite. You may have a vicar watching over you or some other person supervising your work, but you still have far more control over what you will be doing at any time of day than, say, a teacher or bus driver or nurse. The consequence is that, with all that time at your disposal, you think that you have more than you really have and the diary fills up before you know it.

Remember that you have been a layperson and what you are doing now you once did in your leisure time. Now this really is your work. That does not diminish your calling or commitment. It does, though, heighten the responsibility you have to ensure that you work effectively, but also take time off.

So, think of each day as having three sessions – morning, afternoon and evening of, say, four hours each. We live in a culture that is workaholic, but we owe it to those with whom we minister to offer a role-model that values recreation. If we are filling every hour and forever running hither and yon, that is not a good example. So, you are only, except in exceptional circumstances, going to work for two sessions each day. Thus, if you have commitments on Monday morning and afternoon, you should not be working on Monday evening, too. If you are – and sometimes you will be – then you should only do one session on the next day. Figure 3 shows how this works for four days of a hypothetical week.

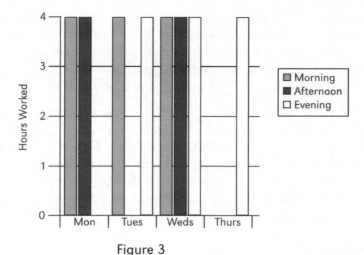

Figure 3

In this way, you make sure that you have slack in your timetable. Doing this has two effects. When a crisis arises, you will have space to deal with it and, when it doesn't, you'll have time to recharge your batteries.

What should I do with my time?

Here before the mountains' grandeur,
Moses waited, nature hushed;
in the stillness and the beauty,
set apart, no longer rushed.
Here he knelt in awe and wonder,
here in glory, God entrusts.

Now wherever God's own presence
breaks into our common ground,
on the mountain, in the temple,
loudly, or without a sound,
there the vision that God offers
challenges all we have found.

Here a different way is offered,
now a fresh resolve is framed,
as the servants of the servant
find that even they are named;
and the call of God is echoed
as each new found life is claimed.*

* Andrew Pratt. Reproduced by permission of Stainer & Bell Ltd.

Personal devotions

With all this opportunity to organize what you do, it is easy to miss what you should do. It was a wise observation, whoever made it, that our own personal devotions are the first thing to get squeezed out of our diaries. The reason is simple. In this you are accountable only to yourself and God, so no one notices if you haven't spent time in devotion.

There are different ways to approach this and, by the time you find yourself in full-time ministry, I hope that you will have developed a pattern that suits you, be it a daily 'office', an early or late prayer time or some other focus. I know of people who pray in their studies and others who pray through some activity, be it walking, knitting or gardening. The important thing is to make the time and guard it well. You need to be in touch with God and yourself.

Study and preparation

It used to be the case that ministers spent every morning in their studies. That's not a bad discipline, but rarely kept. There is a temptation to think that time spent reading or watching a DVD is relaxation. Sometimes it is, but, equally, it can be the means of resourcing yourself so that you communicate, preach and care better.

In this area of your work you will only be caught out if, late on Saturday night, you are wondering what on earth you are going to say on Sunday morning. At this point you are also accountable to your congregation and, if you have not prepared sufficiently well, they will be short-changed. By this I don't just mean that you will have fulfilled your duty by writing an adequate sermon but also that you need to keep up to date with what is happening in society and the news, trying to keep abreast of changes in science, technology and the arts, too, so that you at least have a lay understanding of current debates and the ethics associated with them. Also, of course, it goes without saying, but I'll say it anyway, you need to keep up to date with theology. Some 20 years down the line, the contents of your bookshelves should be at least a little different from those you had when you left training!

Pastoral visits

'The minister never visits us!' It's a common comment and there may be good reason.

I remember seeing the CV of a prospective minister once. It effectively said that he didn't do visits. That raises a question, 'Who is the carer/pastor?'

It has been fashionable to talk of the ministry of all the people, the whole people of God. It is right to underline that all people within the Church have a responsibility for one another. Grouping people together in cells so that those who live near to each other can watch over one another is a good model. Having just three or four households that can raise the alarm when necessary can work wonders in terms of a response to a crisis or alerting others when something goes wrong. In one congregation when such a scheme was implemented, I received calls from two different people when a third went into hospital. One quite elderly woman had cycled to a public phone to let me know. Before the cells were organized I might not have heard about this at all.

Now, while this way of working is valid, it brings into focus the role of the minister. If the recognition or ordination is viewed as purely functional, teleological, then the work the minister does in this model is that of a manager. Added to this may be the role of crisis visitor. So, the minister organizes everyone else. These others visit people and the minister only actively makes visits when called on to do so by one of the other visitors. This might be at a time of illness or bereavement, for instance.

If ministry is viewed as to do with being (ontology), then a visit from the minister is intrinsically different from that of someone who has not been ordained or set aside for this role. Such people who visit may be regarded as representatives of the Church, a friend or a helper. Visiting may be seen as a duty, providing answers. What is clear is that, for some people, regardless of our understanding of ministry, a visit from a minister is seen as distinctive. We cannot get round this even by educating people. It has something to do with a perception of the role rather than the person that is ontological and not in our power to change. Thus, the minister's visit becomes important in its own right, alongside and not replacing visits from any other people in the church.

Such visits may gain significance by being sacramental, such as sharing Communion, or in the expectation of prayer or conversation that is overtly religious. Sometimes just the fact that the minister has visited is enough. Someone may well have felt close to God because you were there even if you did not do very much.

Some warnings, though. This perception of your role is open to abuse. You may be called on more than is reasonable and people may have a heightened perception of your abilities. On the other hand, what you say or do may be received as the ultimate judgment on a matter. It is also possible to wrongly exercise power or control. Equally, a visit from you may not always be welcome or appropriate. You may be perceived as patronizing or intrusive. Your presence may be regarded as a waste of time. Remember, you are not God!

There was a slight pause after I picked up the phone, then a slow intake of breath. No words had been spoken, but I knew who was on the other end. I could feel myself becoming tense. The reaction was quite automatic – there was nothing I could do about it – but my voice had to sound normal, relaxed. Some people do that to me! Past experience says that this is someone I find difficult. It's not the person's fault, it's my problem. I owe them as much care as a minister as anyone else, but they are so easy to avoid!

So, how do we cope with visiting?

Your behaviour will, in part, be influenced by your attitude to those you visit, how you see them and your perception of your role. Is your visit a duty? Do you see Christ in those you visit? Are people problems rather than people?

Visits from a minister are important. Whether they occur in response to a crisis or are of a more regular nature, the administration of them is important.

Administration

Strangely for me, the organization, the administration, really helps. You can go too far, of course. I know some ministers who will spend more time in front of a computer keeping records or filing them away than they ever do in the nitty-gritty of facing people, which is not good, but, nevertheless, the administration can be a real godsend. Although you are not with them, administration is still about the people. Properly used, it can help us to care for them. It can remind us to bother about those we would rather avoid.

'My mother's in a nursing home and no one from the church has been to see her!' The voice of the woman on the phone was angry but also slightly tearful – she was the daughter of a woman who was suffering from dementia. I'd been to see her mother earlier that week. I remembered her. I was also able to refer to my notebook and reassure the woman that I had been, that the church did care. In the notebook was my record of the visit, giving its time, place and purpose. The details of the conversation I'd had were in my head.

What had happened was that the mother had forgotten as soon as I'd left that anyone had been. The staff were too busy to record my presence, but her daughter needed to know that she wasn't alone in bothering about her. Now she did. Relaxed and grateful, we talked a little more. Her burden had been shared. We never met, but it didn't seem to matter.

Since that day, pastoral administration has mattered to me.

Here are some suggestions for ways to keep records that, once set up, can enhance your pastoral ministry. I use a PDA (digital organizer), but you can use paper and it will work in the same way.

First, it is helpful to have a list of all the people for whom you have pastoral responsibility, with their names and addresses. If you can sort these by address (that's where the electronics help), it is invaluable. Every time you make a visit, record the date and purpose. I use the following codes:

- Ch = met at church
- V = visited at home
- C = visited, but they were out (I put a card through the door to let them know I've been)
- Com – home Communion
- Hosp = hospital visit
- F = funeral arrangement
- W = wedding preparation.

You can then set all these details out as shown in the fictional example given in Figure 4.

Surname	First name	Congregation	Street	Number	Code	Date
Smith	Peter	Monmouth	Parker Street	42	hosp	5/7
Jones	Ann	St Brides	John Street	7	V	4/11
Brimelow	Veronica	Monmouth	John Street	9	V	3/2
Pensett	Arthur	Trickmouth	Vernon Street	18	Com	4/7

Figure 4

You may want to add further information as you go, but this serves as the main record of all visits. Over time, you can see which people you have visited most recently and those you have never visited.

A second record is your day-to-day list. In it the same codes can be used, but it is a prompt for the visits that must be made. It consists simply of a name, the code, the date and any other note you need as reminder.

Remember that all these records should be confidential and churches are subject to data protection regulations. You should not hold data without the permission of those to whom it refers and those individuals should be able to have access to what you have recorded. So, be careful not to write anything that you wouldn't want the person to see!

Using these two sets of records as you go about should help you. If you are called to visit one person in a particular road, it is possible to look quickly to see if anyone else lives nearby who you could call on while you are there. A word of warning, though. If two people live next door to each other, it is not always helpful to visit both of them at the same time. It can raise expectations that you may not be able to meet – 'You were with Mrs Smith but you didn't call on me' – and people compare notes – 'the minister was only ten minutes with me, but he spent a whole hour with Mrs Jones!'

E-mails and texts

Increasingly, we communicate by e-mail and send texts. A word of warning: there are a number of potential pitfalls in using these media.

E-mails are sometimes looked on as electronic postcards, flying through the ether and open to scrutiny. This may not be an exact parallel, but remember that, even when you have deleted an e-mail, it may well still be held elsewhere on a server. Messages sent from mobile devices, which appear to be ephemeral, can be held on a service provider's server months after they were deleted from the device that sent them.

Individual e-mails that you send can be shared quickly and easily with other people, simply by being forwarded. While you can do that with a letter, the Internet makes it much easier and potentially more destructive. Imagine you have had an exchange of e-mails with another person. As could happen with a conversation, things have got a bit heated and you've said something that you regret. You then patch things up. You feel better. Later in the day, the person you've been 'talking' with thinks over what you've said and reads the e-mails again. Something of the heat of that moment comes back and they forward an e-mail to a friend, who forwards it to . . . who knows who. So, use e-mails with care. They can be immensely useful, but also potentially very destructive!

Texts often do not carry any personal identification with them. You do not know who sent them unless you recognize the number. It is not always easy to know how to respond appropriately. Neither do most people back-up or keep records of text messages. The same is often true of phone conversations. We do not expect voice conversations to be recorded or kept, but the culture associated with letter writing, from which texts have evolved, is the opposite – the expectation is that these communications will be kept. So, remember to save texts if they are critical and, again, use them with care – they are not as ephemeral as you might think.

Other tasks

Many of the things that ministers do, they don't have to do. There are a lot of administrative tasks that can be done better by someone with secretarial experience and this frees up the minister to fulfil her or his role more effectively.

As a Superintendent Minister, I had to collect a box of papers and letters each time I went to synod. That was part of my role. I was then expected to go through the box and distribute schedules, notices, letters and other papers to a variety of people and congregations. I asked if I could have an assistant and this was arranged. I approached a layperson I knew, in whom I had confidence, who had administrative skills. I still had to collect the box, but then I gave it to her. Two days later, anything that was meant for me was delivered. All the other papers were sent out to the people who needed them.

As time went by, my assistant gradually took on more administrative work, such as writing letters, answering correspondence and helping in all manner of tasks. This meant that I was able to be a minister. Of course I had to let go of some control, some power. I had to risk papers going to the wrong people. That said, some laypeople have skills in this area that a minister may not have! Unltimately, of course, I carried the can for any errors. It was worth it, though. I had a colleague and it freed me up.

You get paid for it, too!

Clergy are paid in different ways and you will need guidance from your church in order to understand the pattern that applies to you.

It is usually understood that clergy, if they are paid at all, are provided with allowances – expenses, if you like – that allow them to live and free them up to do what they are called to do. Often they also live in tied housing. This is a benefit in that there is no need to worry about a mortgage or the cost of moving to a more expensive area. The downside is that the house is never your own. It is open to inspection in the way that a private house never is and you need provision when you retire and leave that tied house. If you receive no income for your ministry, you ought, nevertheless, to receive expenses, even if you later give them back as an offering. Someone following you may not be so well endowed and may need that support. The real cost of ministry ought to be transparent to those who support it.

For all clergy, there are usually extra sources of income – money from weddings and funerals, for instance. In some denominations, such income will go straight to the Church. In others, it is supplementary income for the minister. Whatever the case may be, this income needs to be accounted for, as does income in kind provided for the decoration of a house or running a car, to mention just two examples. There are also a number of legitimate expenses that are tax deductible. The Inland Revenue provides clergy with an extra set of sheets on their self-assessment tax return forms for just these reasons. Take advice from other clergy or an accountant as to what you could claim and what should be disclosed. There are accountants who specialize in working with the clergy and their fees are generally very fair. The Inland Revenue's staff are also available to deal with queries. The time taken to keep your taxes in order will be repaid by knowing that you will not be billed for late payments or pay too much tax.

Using your time effectively

You will have plenty of calls on your time. The important thing is to be discerning. Continually refer back to your sense of calling, your vocation. Ask yourself if what you are being asked to do aligns with what you believe God has called you to do. Then, beyond that, be honest about your own gifts, skills and ability. You are unlikely to be brilliant at everything, whatever your congregation might think or expect. Their picture of 'what ministers do' will be a collage of what all the ministers they have known have done! Don't be afraid to say, 'No'.

Summary

1. Your time is your own. Use it wisely.
2. Know what is expected of you.
3. Study and preparation is part of your work.
4. Don't forget God – remember your devotions.
5. Care for people, even those you don't care for!
6. Keep good records.

Looking ahead

- Learn how to be helped.
- Share your load.
- Remember your calling and revisit it regularly.

Chapter 13
Beyond the Church

A letter flopped on to my doormat. It had been hand delivered and I opened it with interest. My senior steward had tendered his resignation. He said that he couldn't work with someone who was 'political', who criticized the Establishment and ridiculed the armed forces. That was the gist of it anyway. This tirade had been sparked off by a letter that I'd written to the local paper making a comment on some action taken by the then government in relation to some international crisis. I thought that I had simply brought a gospel perspective to the debate. He had read so much more into it and had embroidered his perception of what I had said with his own prejudices. I was new to that church and he hardly knew me.

I can't remember the exact circumstances behind the letter that I wrote, but I don't think I've changed so much I wouldn't write in that manner again. Maybe my language would be more temperate, but I doubt it!

I called on him. I listened to his point of view. In doing so, I understood him much better. Then I asked him to listen to me and, to give him credit, he did. We agreed on a cooling-off period. He withdrew his resignation, we agreed to differ on this issue and, over time, became good friends and allies.

I tell this story as a warning. If your call to ministry has an element in it that I would characterize as 'prophetic', beware. What you see as clear-cut and scriptural may be offensive to others. It is my view that apartheid was an abomination, yet those who worked against it were labelled as terrorists by the British government at the time. Preaching on this to an ecumenical congregation caused one person to walk out, as I metioned earlier (p. 24). The gospel is not always palatable, sometimes it is scandalous and, if you intend to point that out to people, you have to be prepared for the fact that you may not be popular.

Priest or prophet?

It seems to me that there are at least four callings to ministry – there may be more. One focuses on preaching, teaching and the sacraments within the Church. Another is heavily pastorally based. A third looks outwards, to evangelize and communicate to those outside or on the fringes of the Church. The last looks at the world and offers a Christian critique of what is seen.

All are necessary and we may embody all of them to a greater or lesser extent. The last is the most dangerous one. In some contexts, it can lead to martyrdom and I am not being melodramatic in saying that. We only have to look to the example of Archbishop Oscar Romero to realize that criticism of political structures from a Christian perspective can bring persecution. Tragically, he was shot in church while celebrating Mass after having criticized the government.

> Seeing salvation, a vision of heaven:
> doors to God's glory are flung open wide;
> here in the face of the hungry or homeless
> Jesus is present and hope can reside.
>
> This unexpected, though God-given presence,
> stark, cold reality captures the eye;
> surely this poverty cannot encompass
> Jesus' divinity, prophecy's sigh?
>
> Here in simplicity, here on the pavement,
> under the arches, down rain-sodden roads
> Jesus is walking, through saddened eyes staring,
> loving the broken and easing their loads.*

The moment we move outside the confines of the institution of the Church, in whatever context, we may be criticized. Murder is the extreme response, the comment that 'we pay you and have a right to see you' is another. Sometimes this latter response is valid. It is easy for dissatisfied ministers to lose themselves in what their congregations regard as peripheral activities. It can be a way of running away from commitment, responsibility and accountability. We need to be sure about what we are doing, certain of our call and cognisant of our motives when we work outside the Church. For some, this distinctive work is best delineated by an understanding of different forms of ministry. The worker-priest movement in France in the 1950s was one such response. The move to distinguish between the roles of presbyteral and diaconal ministries is a more recent symptom of the same need. These distinctions safeguard practitioners and signify the worth of a particular calling to the wider Church. Nevertheless, for the foreseeable future, ministers, in the generic sense, will find that some of the activities in which they are engaged will not have clear-cut boundaries and may cause friction or resentment among those with whom they are appointed to minister on a day-to-day basis.

A full-time chaplain has recognition. A part-time chaplain is sometimes expected to be full-time in two places at once. Indeed, in some situations, the

---

* Andrew Pratt. Reproduced by permission of Stainer & Bell Ltd.

Church may place chaplains in institutions that do not recognize them. In such instances, it is necessary to clarify what is expected of the role.

Some of the problems associated with part-time working can be ameliorated at least by being public about what is being done and arriving at agreed boundaries for the work. If you are always 'at the hospital on Monday', then at least you can't realistically be expected to be somewhere else on that day. Occasional part-time actions are more difficult to justify and accommodate. Sometimes we need to explain what we are doing to those we are accountable to, those who appointed us, manage us, pay us or expect us to visit them.

With all these pitfalls, you might be asking, 'Is it worth doing anything peripheral to the main focus of our calling?' The answer is an unequivocal 'Yes'.

Chaplaincy

It was 2.30 in the morning when the phone rang. The nurse was calm yet sounded tired and at her wits' end. 'Can you come to Ward 2, we have a patient who is dying.' My own bed was more enticing at that moment than sitting by someone else's, but this is a responsibility that comes with being a hospital chaplain. In half an hour, I was at the hospital. The person who I'd been called to see went on to live two more days, but, there I was, at the hospital, at three in the morning.

The nurse who had called knew that the woman was dying, but also knew her death was not imminent – sometimes you do, sometimes you don't. So why had I been called? Nurses are human. This one had been acting as a referee rather than being able to care for the patient.

The woman concerned had been ill for some time and had been cared for by her daughter and son-in-law – a common enough scenario. Her health deteriorated and she was admitted to hospital. That night, her son and daughter-in-law, who lived some way off, had been called and came. The family who had been caring for the woman were also there and resented the other couple. The other couple felt guilty for not having been there. In the resulting tension between them, they were arguing and sniping at each other across their mother's bed. The nurse had been trying to care for the dying woman while simultaneously trying to both comfort and calm the relatives. They were not up to being calmed!

So, why was I there? The nurse apologized and said that she just needed help managing the situation. Both the son and daughter had a right to be with their mother, but, if they were there together, they fought. My task was to keep them apart without it being obvious!

To this end, I suggested that it would be helpful to get to know them. Perhaps in turn they'd come to the canteen and have a cup of tea. We did this until 8 a.m. By then, some of the tension was beginning to ease and we all went and had breakfast together. Meanwhile, the nurse had been able to do her job better and the brother and sister had remembered that that's what they were to each other, whatever differences there had been. I'm sure they rowed again, I'm sure the solution wasn't permanent, but their mother had been allowed a little more peace and dignity as she moved towards death.

I couldn't help thinking that I hadn't expected this when I became a hospital chaplain!

In a book like this, there is insufficient space to consider all the ramifications of different forms of chaplaincy. Suffice it to say, they are all vital to their own constituencies and give opportunities for ministry that are both valuable and diverse.

A word of warning, though. A young man on a talent show scouting for a new 'star' for a West End musical was asked, 'Are you in this for the fame or do you want the job?' It is a good question for a potential chaplain, too.

Chaplains may appear to be in fields that appear 'glamorous' simply because they are different. Riding on a tank across a desert may appeal to some. Ministering to a young man or woman who has experienced the horror of seeing their best friend's limbs being blown off and wakes up screaming with nightmares is altogether different. Mixing with highly qualified professionals in an educational or medical setting may have its attractions. Being on a panel dismissing a colleague or ministering to someone who has been accused of abuse may be rather more taxing. So, ask yourself whether you really want the nitty-gritty of this responsibility or is it just attractive because it seems different or exciting?

Conflict

I and my Anglican colleague were chaplains to a local hospital. The hospital was due to close. The land and buildings were to be sold to raise money for an extension to another larger hospital in the healthcare trust.

Due to an oversight on our part, we both went off on holiday simultaneously during August. When we returned, one of the wards was empty, its doors held closed by a heavy chain and padlock. We knew that, eventually, all the wards would close. No one had told us about this impending closure. When we enquired. it became clear that the staff, though they were careful not to be critical, had not been told either. The ward had been closed and emptied in the space of a week.

All well and good? Well, no. The ward had been occupied by long-stay patients, some of whom had been there for 30 years. They had had no more notice than the staff of the fact that they were, in the jargon of the day, to be 'decanted' to another hospital nearly 30 miles away. This had the consequence of disorientating them. We had noticed that, at one point, when the ward had been reorganized, just moving them from one end to the other had been upsetting. This move was far worse, detaching them from their community and any friends or family who visited.

On paper, chaplains simply minister to the patients. In this situation, however, my colleague and I felt that it was appropriate for us to put aside any contractual obligations of our role and 'become ministers'. We did what we could to determine who had been responsible for managing the change and how it had taken place. We sought facts, not hearsay. It was quite clear that what had happened had been driven by economics and took no account of the welfare of the people the hospital trust had in its care.

We arranged a meeting with the Chief Executive of the trust and, together, put forward an ultimatum. Either the further movements of patients and staff – this movement was not likely to be stopped completely – was managed with regard to giving notice to and preparing those involved – a process that we knew would take a minimum of several months – or we would go public. We pointed out that we were in a privileged position in that we, unlike the staff, were not reliant on the trust for our employment and income.

We both remained as chaplains and oversaw the gradual closure of the hospital over a number of months.

When you are involved in formal chaplaincy situations or working in contexts that are not those of the institutional Church, there are times when you will find yourself in situations of conflict. Such conflict can come about because you are operating in a secular environment, but, in essence, you are still, or ought to be, called by God, a minister and in some way separate. On the one hand, the context is one in which you are accountable to secular authorities that set parameters within which you are meant to work, people to whom you are accountable, tasks you are expected to perform, but, on the other, you operate according to an unspoken ethic that carries you in other times in your Christian ministry. It is dangerous and hypocritical to put aside that ethic simply because you are operating in a secular situation.

The media

How to handle it

I answered the phone and a voice said, 'We understand that the Church has made some comments relating to human sexuality. As a minister, what do you think about this?'

Ministers, as representatives of the Church, are sometimes called on by the media for comment. The temptation is to answer the question. In some instances, particularly if you know the person who is calling you, that may be entirely safe and appropriate. More often, though, it is not. Words can be taken out of context and damage both you and the Church.

So, what do you do? Some might counsel you simply to say, 'No comment', whatever the question. This can sometimes be as damaging as making a comment, however. Imagine the following scenario. The local press ring up asking your opinion about the fact that a racist candidate is standing in your local elections. 'No comment,' you say. Really? Imagine the headlines. 'Racist stands for election to local council – church has nothing to say.'

So how can we best cope with this sort of request. Here we can learn from politicians. First, underline the fact that we are willing to make a response, but negotiate when and how that will be. For printed media, a written response is best and, if you are concerned that you might be misrepresented, place the condition that it must be printed in full with no additions or deletions. That may mean you don't see your name in print, but, equally, they can't say you made no comment – you have it on record that you did.

Only in extreme circumstances are you likely to go on television. Radio is more likely. Arrange a time when you will either go into a studio or be interviewed over the telephone. Again, it is sensible to make notes and, without sounding stilted, use them as a guide as to what you want to say. Be aware that what you say may be edited, so ask to be informed as to what will be broadcast before it goes out. You may not be able to change it, but at least you will know what is coming.

If all of this sounds very defensive, it is founded on a knowledge and respect for journalists and others in the media who have a job to do. How they present you will depend on their judgment as to what will go best in the particular medium in which they are involved. Soundbites are easier to listen to than long, involved arguments or sentences with lots of clauses.

Broadcasting

If you are fortunate enough to be asked to broadcast in your own right, then there are still some ground rules to be borne in mind. You will be working with professionals who are doing this regularly, if not for a living. They know what works best with their particular audience, so listen to their advice. You may have ideas that are novel and they may well be willing to listen to them, but remember that the reason they're novel – in the sense of 'not found in that particular medium' – may well be because they have already been tried and failed.

Remember also that broadcasting is regulated and subject to listeners' and viewers' expectations. What will be acceptable on local radio may not work for a larger-scale religious broadcaster or national television.

With all of these opportunities, work hard to build good relationships with your producer, interviewer and others with whom you are working. This is very much a team exercise and, though you may have been asked because you are an 'expert' in your subject, you need everyone else for that expertise to be presented well.

This is an area in which ministers do not always shine. They think they know all about communication, yet they are so used to working on their own that they find taking advice or direction difficult.

Taking a lead

When AIDS/HIV was first in the news, it was presented in very negative terms. The Church was as bad, if not worse, than the media in how it dealt with people living with HIV. There was a moral high ground to be won and some in the Church were determined to stand on it.

My training and work before I entered the ministry had been in the biological sciences. My first interest in AIDS/HIV, therefore, was from that angle. I began to read about the syndrome in popular scientific literature. It quickly became clear that we were dealing with a virus that infected anyone who received blood products or body fluids containing the virus.

Unless you come from a particularly blinkered theological perspective, viral infections are, in themselves, neutral, even if the means of contracting them might sometimes, for some people, be open to question. Thus, those who had already contracted the virus warranted care, particularly Christian care in the light of Jesus' attitude to people he came across who were ill. It was not the people who were ill that he judged most stridently, but those who would disable or exclude them from their communities because of an illness or disability.

The pattern seemed clear to me. Something needed to be done and my background and expertise gave me the tools to begin to act.

I knew a doctor working with people with HIV. She was also involved with people publishing a networking magazine. I began to write in it. Within the Church, I started to raise awareness of the issue with those who had responsibility at a national level for this sort of issue. The person concerned was all too willing to have an informed enthusiast who was willing to carry this flag.

Eventually I had quite a lot of responsibility delegated to me to speak on this issue, work ecumenically and raise informed awareness more generally. All the while, carers and researchers were doing the real work. Eventually, I felt that the issue was on the Church's agenda and it was time for me to leave things in the hands of people better informed and more capable than myself to move things forward. With growing awareness and education there was less judgment and more compassion abroad in the Church.

It is possible to take up issues like this from time to time in order to have a prophetic voice within the Church. Unfortunately, the role of the prophet, of calling people back to God, is not yet redundant and it is often needed within the institution of the Church.

This can never just be a hobby-horse, though. You must be well informed in order to talk competently with professionals in the field as well as being able to bring theological reflection to bear on the issue you are addressing. Doing this, even well, can bring you into conflict with your own congregation. The comfortable never like to be unsettled.

This role is not for everyone. Some will never have either the need or the expertise to take up such a struggle. Know, however, that you will be neglecting an important part of your ministry if you do feel that need and you have that expertise and then do nothing.

Politics

This man had learnt too much, it seemed,
knew ways of right and wrong,
his ear attuned to righteousness
sensed discord in their song.

The politicians and the priests
were threatened by this choice;
The hypocrites would silence him,
and still we shun his voice.*

* Andrew Pratt. Reproduced by permission of Stainer & Bell Ltd.

'Can I say something about this, minister?'

It was a retired working man speaking. He was a steward in the local chapel. He and his neighbours had had a letter about a proposed new road. If it went ahead, it would cut the community in half and the links between one side and the other were already, to say the least, inadequate. He wanted to ask the support of the chapel in making political representation to the local authority about the new road.

You can't simply go ahead and put the chapel name, and your own as minister, to such representations unless the people are with you. With the best will in the world and the most satisfactory of motives, they could rightly accuse you of misrepresenting them.

So we talked with the people and it was their decision that a letter, duly approved, should go from the church to the Local Authority with my signature as minister. Letters went to and fro. Public meetings were held. Eventually, the plans were changed. The chapel, small though it was, had had a significant role in speaking for the community.

If you believe in the people with whom you are ministering, and the community of which you are a part, then you cannot but be interested and involved in politics at one level or another. As a representative within the community you may be asked to be chaplain to a mayor or organize civic services. Remember in all these that, having such a representative role, it is incumbent on you not to misrepresent those with whom you minister or the Church that you also represent.

Integrity

Always be true to your own integrity and open about what you believe. An example will illustrate this point.

I was approached by an officer of the local branch of the British Legion, asking if I would be willing to preach at their Armistice Day service. I would have had no objection to doing this and felt honoured to be asked. There was just one thing. So, I wrote back saying that I was most honoured and willing to accept, but I thought they ought to know that I am a pacifist and an active member of the Methodist Peace Fellowship and the Fellowship of Reconciliation. I had no qualms about being involved in such an event – after all, none of us want war. They did not feel the same and the invitation was withdrawn. I had to be honest to be fair to them.

Summary

1. Ministry does not just take place within a church, but, equally, other activities should not be a way of escaping responsibilities.
2. Outside activities can bring conflict in a variety of ways. Some of this can be mitigated by first seeking the agreement of your church or congregation.
3. Some outside commitments may seem glamorous – the reality can be quite different.
4. Beware part-time commitments that actually take all your time.
5. Your own theological integrity and calling may cut across the expectations and even the contractual obligations of some secular appointments.
6. Treat the media with care and respect.
7. Do not speak as if on behalf of the Church when you are expressing your own opinion.

Looking ahead

- Reflect on your calling regularly.
- Should you be speaking prophetic words or taking prophetic action?
- Should you be active outside the Church?
- Are you escaping your responsibilities by working outside the Church?

Chapter 14
Go into all the world

Jesus' words are awe-inspiring to say the least, so let's get back to basics.

A crisis kicked in when I was three years into ministry. I went back to full-time teaching for a spell. An appointment in a church was open to me and I nearly didn't go. The trouble was that this thing that we variously refer to as a calling or vocation persisted. God would not let me go. There was a feeling that, if I didn't give it another go, I'd regret it forever and always wonder what would have happened.

That was me. I know other ministers who have left ministry. Some have become campaigning atheists, some are cynical, others are comfortable in another context. The way through for some has been a different way of exercising their vocation – in the media or education, for instance – but still very committed.

Ministry is not easy. Sometimes it seems impossible. So, how do we survive, year in year out? It is a cliché, though true, that this is not our work but God's and our work is done in his strength, not our own. Nevertheless, rather like riding a bicycle, there are ways of making the journey easier on ourselves.

Be yourself

If in ministry or any other situation, you are acting out a part or playing a game all the time, it will soon take its toll. Either you will begin to show symptoms of stress and irritability or your guard will drop and you will say or do something that you regret.

There are so many different roles that the minister is meant to fulfil, however, that there is bound to be a bit of play-acting involved. If you have conducted a funeral and been appropriately involved, it will be emotionally and, perhaps, spiritually and physically exhausting. If you then need to go on to a wedding interview, a business meeting or a church celebration, all those feelings will have to be kept on hold until you can give expression to them or let them go in counsel and supervision or prayer. In the end, though, you still need to be yourself, to find a way of dealing with your feelings, not just suppressing them. It's no good thinking, 'Well, it's just this once', because it will happen again and the unresolved tension will build up over time. For these situations you need support structures (see Chapter 1). Make sure that they are in place and use all the support you can get.

The need to act reduces when you are able to admit who you are to the people around you, with whom you are ministering. How true to yourself you are being you can sometimes monitor with a journal. Ask yourself, and be honest, was the last sermon you preached one you were wholly committed to? If it wasn't, what had you said that you were doubtful about or didn't believe. If you find that you are repeating the doctrines of the Church without much conviction, ask yourself why you're preaching like this. Is it a theme you have to address? If not, then maybe you should avoid it. If it is one that you need to confront, do you not think that members of your congregation might also have doubts? Could sharing this with them be reassuring rather than undermine your faith or theirs?

In a meeting after that funeral, could you admit that the day has been difficult? You'd be amazed how understanding people can be. Yes, there will always be some who will come back with comments such as, 'If you can't stand the heat, keep out of the kitchen.' Others will recognize something of the pressure that you experience and a few will be understanding – asking how you are, what sort of a day you've had. The genuine will ask really wanting to know and to share your burden with you.

Throughout my ministry, there have been places and people I have been able to go to – a comfortable home, a café, the occupational therapy department of a hospital where I was chaplain – where I knew I could be myself, let off steam and be understood. They are special, a sort of sanctuary.

Take time off

Remember that there is a difference between being a Christian, which is full-time and life-long, and being employed by the Church, which is, in many ways, like any other job. Like any other job, you need to rest from it sometimes! You are not at people's beck and call, though you should be available. The first speaks of dropping everything at the least call on your time. Being available means that people can call on you to minister with and to them, but you set your own priorities and boundaries.

A pattern of rest time that is almost non-negotiable is essential. I say 'almost' here because crises and emergencies do occur, but make sure that is really what they are, not just an excuse to feel wanted again. For some people, taking time off is harder than working.

Take some time in each day and at least a day in each week away from work and calls on your time. Some denominations encourage time away each quarter, say two or three days. If you have a family, and even if you don't, getting away may be financially impossible, but you can at least indicate to people that this is your space and it's work-free. Find time for reflection, too, so that you can reassess your vocation and direction in company with a spiritual director or on your own. Also, from time to time, take a holiday. My own denomination has a peculiar structure to its year, beginning in September. September and October can be hectic, so a week off in late October or November is a godsend. You come back refreshed for Advent and ready for Christmas. Then, instead of arriving at the festive season worn out, you might actually enjoy it and that's no bad thing!

> Each person needs a stopping place
> here in the movement of these days;
> a space, somewhere to find ourselves,
> amid this curling, madding maze.
>
> Caught in this moment let us rest
> and find in silence God is good;
> that in this whirl, this twist of pain
> the love of God is understood.
>
> Within this instant let us stay
> the driven urgency and press,
> the onward rush, the ceaseless train,
> the reason for our fear and stress.
>
> Be still, and know that God is here,
> let love enfold and grace becalm;
> yes, rest awhile, and rest in God,
> and feel the spirit's soothing balm.

Vocation

Why on earth do we go on with the task of ministry from year to year? As a teacher I was conscious that some staff members were working their time out. I suppose there are folk like that in most walks of life. It is no different in ministry and, yet, in a way it is.

Ministry is a mix of work and vocation, as we have seen. The best scenario is that the two coalesce. The content of our vocation and our expression of it will probably be different in detail from that of other ministers we know, but I begin to get wary when what I am doing has no relation to my vocation.

So, every so often, there is a need to step back and ask yourself again, 'What is the nature of my calling? To what am I called? How is that calling to be expressed?' As you answer these questions, you need to be honest about what you are doing and how you are doing it.

At one stage in my ministry I was going into seven schools every half term to take assemblies. What did that have to do with my vocation? The question had to be asked and answered. The people to whom I was accountable, with whom I ministered, needed to know why so much time was being spent in schools. Was it an escape back into what was, for me, safe territory? Was it a genuine opportunity for mission in the wide sense of that word, ministering on the edge of the Church? If that was so, was that a legitimate role for me? I was able to give satisfactory answers to these questions. If I had not been able to do so, I would have had to reassess what I was doing in relation to my vocation and make some changes.

As we move through our lives, the same vibrant sense of call that we once felt may well find its expression in a variety of situations and circumstances. However, we must be sure at each step of the way that we are keeping integrity with ourselves, the God who has called us and those with whom we serve.

If the vocation loses its vibrancy, then, again, we need to be honest to God and ourselves. People do leave ministry and find other equally fulfilling ways through their lives. So may we. We may need to.

The will to go on

If the vocation is still there and there is work to do, then we need to do it. My own experience has shown me that ministry is the most fulfilling, most highly privileged way of living a life that I know.

That is a strong, positive statement and it may not always feel like that. Indeed, in all honesty, it has not always felt like that for me. So, I'd better explain why I make this claim.

Ministry is one of the few occupations that offers an immense amount of space for self-determination. Yes, there are expectations and demands, but, on many mornings, I can ask myself, 'What shall I do today?' and answer to my own satisfaction.

There are few occupations that are as widely varied from day to day as this one. Ministry deals with life and death, crisis and community, alienation and joy. It brings you into contact with different people, doing different jobs and none. Listening pastorally is like reading biographies, but far more real and vivid for we rarely meet biographers face to face. I've milked cows and talked trains. I've heard about the building of the Canadian Pacific railway from a navvy. I've sat while a young woman, near to death, has taken stock of her life and relationships, needing to resolve things before she no longer could. Then

I witnessed the reconciliation, the glow of love and satisfaction shared with her father with whom she fell out years before. I have been with parents revelling in the life of their first-born and those grieving the loss of twins at birth. The list is as endless as the people I've met and will meet.

Then, looking out at a congregation gathered for worship, you realize that you have shared intimate, painful, real, moments with them; that you know more about all of them than they know about each other; that you cherish and treasure the privacy and privilege of that knowledge; that you are very like the parent of children. Then you realize that some of the people looking at you are under 4 years old and some are over 94. You know them and they trust you. You feel intimately part of a community in which you are loved as a leader. That is not too sentimental – at best that is how it can become. There is no greater gift, no more fulfilling a calling, than ministering with the people of God.

When I remember all that, the cantankerous, awkward, difficult person I can sometimes be mellows a little. For I see in others my own failings and hope they don't always see mine in me!

God marks no ending, only new beginnings,
until the consummation of our lives;
God keeps no count of losses, nor of winnings:
we move through grace, the holy spirit thrives.

So as we go beyond this time, this setting,
rememb'ring all the laughter and the tears;
we go with God in faith, so not regretting
the moments shared, the hopes, the dreams, the fears.

Though parted for a while, we travel onward,
not knowing what the future has in store.
This phase will close, the spirit draws us forward,
we've tasted love, but God has promised more!*

* Andrew Pratt. Reproduced by permission of Stainer & Bell Ltd.

Resources

Unattributed poems within this book are written by the author.

Chapter 1

Baptism, Eucharist and Ministry: The agreed text, Geneva, World Council of Churches, 1982.

Beasley-Murray, P., *Anyone for Ordination*, Tunbridge Wells, MARC, 1993.

Croft, S., and Walton, R., *Learning for Ministry*, London and Peterborough, Church House Publishing in collaboration with the Methodist Publishing House, 2005.

Foskett J., Lyall D., *Helping the Helpers: Supervision and pastoral care*, London, SPCK, 1988.

Ison, D. (ed.), *The Vicar's Guide*, London, Church House Publishing, 2005.

Jacobs, M., *Holding in Trust: The appraisal of ministry*, London, SPCK, 1989.

Luscombe, P., and Shreeve, E., *What is a Minister?*, Peterborough, Epworth, 2002.

Witcombe, J. (ed.), *The Curate's Guide*, London, Church House Publishing, 2005.

Chapter 2

Ammerman, N., Carroll, J. W., Dudley, C. S., and McKinney, W. (eds), *Studying Congregations: A new handbook*, Nashville, TN, Abingdon, 1998.

Archbishop's Commission on Urban Priority Areas, *Faith in the City*, London, Church House Publishing, 1985.

Barnes, M., *Religions in Conversation*, London, SPCK, 1989.

Bennett, C., *Community Work with People of Other Faiths*, Durham, Churches' Community Work Alliance.

Cameron, H., Richter, P., Davies, D., and Ward, F. (eds), *Studying Local Churches: A handbook*, London, SCM, 2005.

Cockerell, D., *Beginning Where We Are: A theology of parish ministry*, London, SCM, 1989.

Commission on Urban Life and Faith, *Faithful Cities: A call for celebration, vision and justice*, Peterborough and London, Methodist Publishing House and Church House Publishing, 2006.

Green, L., *Urban Ministry and the Kingdom of God*, London, SPCK, 2003.

Lartey, E. Y., *Pastoral Theology in an Intercultural World*, Peterborough, Epworth, 2006.

Methodist Church, *Presence*, Methodist Church, London, 2004.

Chapter 3

Bell, J. L., *The Singing Thing: A case for congregational song*, Glasgow, Wild Goose Publications, 2000.

Bell, J. L., *The Singing Thing Too*, GIA, Chicago, 2007.

Brueggemann, W., *Finally Comes the Poet: Daring speech for proclamation*, Minneapolis, MN, Fortress Press, 1989.

Duck, R. C., *Finding Words for Worship: A guide for leaders*, Louisville, KY, Westminster John Knox Press, 1995.

Eslinger, R. L., *Narrative and Imagination: Preaching the worlds that shape us*, Minneapolis, MN, Fortress Press, 1995.

Haugen, M., *To Serve as Jesus Did*, Chicago, IL, GIA, 2005.

McEwen D., Pinsent, P., Pratt I., and Seddon V., *Making Liturgy: Creating rituals for worship and life*, London, Canterbury Press, 2001.

Schmidt, C. J., *Too Deep for Words: A theology of liturgical expression*, Louisville, KY, Westminster John Knox Press, 2002.

Schultze Q. J., *High-tech Worship? Using presentational technologies wisely*, Grand Rapids, MI, Baker Academic, 2004.

Townsend, M., *Thinking Things Through 6: Sacraments*, Peterborough, Epworth, 1999.

Ward, H., and Wild J., (eds), *Human Rites: Worship resources for an age of change*, London, Mowbray, 1995.

White, S., *Groundwork of Christian Worship*, Peterborough, Epworth, 1997.

Wren, B., *Praying Twice: The music and words of congregational song*, Louisville, KY, Westminster John Knox Press, 2000.

Wootton, J., *Introducing a Practical Feminist Theology of Worship*, London, Sheffield, Academic Press, 2000.

Chapter 4

Avis, P., *A Ministry Shaped by Mission*, London, T. & T. Clark, 2005.

Baelz, P., and Jacob, W. (eds), *Ministers of the Kingdom: Exploration in non-stipendiary ministry*, London, CIO, 1985.

Baptism, Eucharist and Ministry: The agreed text, Geneva, World Council of Churches, 1982.

Bowden, A., *Ministry in the Countryside: A model for the future*, London, Continuum. 2003.

Bruce, J. E., *Proclaiming the Scandal: Reflections on postmodern ministry*, Philadelphia, PA, Trinity Press International, 2000.

Bunting, I., *Models of Ministry: Managing the Church today*, New York, Grove Press, 1993.

Campbell, J. M., *Being Biblical*, London, United Reformed Church, 2003.

Clark, D., *Breaking the Mould of Christendom: Kingdom community, diaconal church and the liberation of the laity*, Peterborough, Epworth, 2005.

Croft, S., *Ministry in Three Dimensions*, London, Darton, Longman & Todd, 1999.

Cross, A. R., Thompson, P. E., and Packer, J. I., *Baptist Sacramentalism*, Milton Keynes, Paternoster, 2003.

Francis, J., and Francis, L. J., *Tentmaking: Perspectives on self-supporting ministry*, Leominster, Gracewing, 1998.

Shreeve, E., and Luscombe, P. (eds), *What is a Minister?*, Peterborough, Epworth, 2002.

Chapter 5

Baillie, J., *Baptism and Conversion*, Oxford, Oxford University Press, 1964.

Baptism, Eucharist and Ministry: The agreed text, Geneva, World Council of Churches, 1982.

Beasley-Murray, G. R., *Baptism in the New Testament*, London, Macmillan, 1963.

Best, T., and Heller, D., (eds) *Becoming a Christian: The ecumenical implications of our common baptism*, Geneva, World Council of Churches, 1999.

Buchanan, C., *A Case for Infant Baptism*, New York, Grove Press, 1973.

Cross, A. R., Thompson, P. E., and Packer, J. I., *Baptist Sacramentalism*, Milton Keynes, Paternoster, 2003.

Fiddes, P., *Reflections on the Water*, Oxford, Regents Park College, 1998.

Kennedy, D. J., and Tovey, P., *Methodist and United Reformed Church Worship: Baptism and Communion in two 'free' churches*, New York, Grove Press, 1992.

Macquarrie, J., *A Guide to the Sacraments*, London, SCM, 1997.

Owen, C., Buchanan, C., and Wright, A., *Reforming Infant Baptism*, London, Hodder & Stoughton, 1990.

Spinks, B. D., *Reformation and Modern Rituals and Theologies of Baptism: From Luther to contemporary practices*, Aldershot, Ashgate Publishing, 2006.

Tidball, D., *Baptist Basics*, Baptist Union of Great Britain (pamphlet).

Townsend, M., *Thinking Things Through 6: Sacraments*, Peterborough, Epworth, 1999.

United Reformed Church, *Orders of Services for Baptism, Confirmation, Thanksgiving for the Birth of a Child, Renewal of Baptism Promises*, Oxford, Oxford University Press, 1990.

Chapter 6

Baptism, Eucharist and Ministry: The agreed text, Geneva, World Council of Churches, 1982.

Cross, A. R., Thompson, P. E., and Packer, J. I., *Baptist Sacramentalism*, Milton Keynes, Paternoster, 2003.

Faith and Order Committee, Methodist Church, *His Presence Makes the Feast: Holy Communion in the Methodist Church*, Peterborough, MPH, 2003.

Gordon-Taylor, B., and Jones, S., *Celebrating the Eucharist*, London, SPCK, 2005.

Guidelines on the Lord's Supper, London, United Reformed Church, 1983.

Kreider, E., *Given for You: A fresh look at Communion*, Nottingham, Inter-Varsity Press, 1998.

O'Malley, B., *A Celtic Eucharist*, London, Canterbury Press, 2001.

Macquarrie, J., *A Guide to the Sacraments*, London, SCM, 1997.

Miller, C., *Praying the Eucharist: Reflections on the eucharistic experience of God*, London, SPCK, 1995.

Townsend, M., *Thinking Things Through 6: Sacraments*, Peterborough, Epworth, 1999.

Chapter 7

Chambers, P., and Blows, D., *Made in Heaven? Ministry with those intending marriage*, London, SPCK, 1988.

Dominian, J., *Marriage, Faith and Love*, London, Darton, Longman & Todd, 1981.

Dormor, D., *Just Cohabiting? The Church, sex and getting married*, London, Darton, Longman & Todd, 2004.

Goodacre, N. W., and Watson, N., *Making Marriage Work: Meditations on 1 Corinthians 13*, London, Canterbury Press, 1996.

Green, W., *The Future of the Family*, London, Mowbray, 1984.

Macquarrie, J., *A Guide to the Sacraments*, London, SCM, 1997.

Oppenheimer, H., *Marriage*, London, Mowbray, 1990.

Step Carefully: Preparation for marriage where there are children from a previous relationship, London, Methodist Church House, 2001.

Thatcher, A., *Marriage after Modernity*, London, Sheffield Academic Press, 1999.

Thatcher, A., *Celebrating Christian Marriage*, London, T. & T. Clark, 2001.

Chapter 8

Abrams, R., *When Parents Die: Learning to live with the loss of a parent*, London, Routledge, 1999.

Ainsworth-Smith I., and Speck P., *Letting Go: Caring for the dying and bereaved*, London, SPCK, 1982.

Bentley, J., Best, A., and Hunt, J., *Funerals: A guide: Prayers, readings, hymns*, London, Hodder & Stoughton, 1994.

Bell, J. L., *The Love which Heals: A service of grieving and gratitude for those who have been recently bereft*, Glasgow, Wild Goose Publications, 2000.

Billings, A., *Dying and Grieving*, London, SPCK, 2002.

Dickenson, D., and Johnson, M., (eds), *Death, Dying and Bereavement*, London, Sage, 1993.

Dobson, M., and Pratt, A., *Poppies and Snowdrops*, Peterborough, Inspire, 2006.

Duff, W., *Children and Bereavement*, London, Church House Publishing, 2003.

Kirkpatrick, B., *Going Forth*, London, Darton, Longman & Todd, 1997.

Kohner, N., and Henley, A., *When a Baby Dies: The experience of late miscarriage, stillbirth and neonatal death*, London, Routledge, 2001.

Orbach, A., *Life, Psychotherapy and Death: The end of our exploring*, London, Jessica Kingsley, 1999.

Scott, D., *Coping with Suicide*, London, Sheldon Press, 1989.

Chapter 9

Christou, S., *Evangelism and Collaborative Ministry in the Local Church*, Phoenix Books, 2004.

Clark, N., *Team Building: A practical guide for trainers*, Maidenhead, McGraw-Hill, 1994.

Cormack, D., *Team Spirit: People working with people*, Tunbridge Wells, MARC Europe, 1987.

Cornelias, H., and Faire, S., *Everyone Can Win: How to resolve conflict*, London, Simon & Schuster, 1989.

Darswell, A., *Ministry Leadership Teams: Theory and practice in effective collaborative ministry*, New York, Grove Press, 2003.

Greenwood, R., *The Ministry Team Handbook*, London, SPCK, 2000.

Handy, C., *Understanding Voluntary Organisations*, London, Penguin, 1988.

Nelson, J., and Harvey-Jones, J., *Management and Ministry: Appreciating contemporary issues*, London, Canterbury Press, 1997.

Chapter 10

Mabey, C., Mayon-White, W.M. (Ed.), *Managing Change*, Sage Publications (Published in association with The Open University) 1993.

Newton, R., *Managing Change Step by Step: All You Need to Build a Plan and Make it Happen*, Prentice Hall, 2007.

Murren, D., *Leadershift: How to Lead Your Church into the 21st Century by Managing Change*, Ventura, Regal Books, 1993.

Gann, N., *Managing change in voluntary organizations: a guide to practice*, Milton Keynes, Open University Press, 1996.

McLaren, B.D., *The church on the other side: doing ministry in the postmodern matrix*, Michigan, Zondervan, 2000.

Thorogood, B., *No abiding city: change and changelessness in the church*, London, SCM Press, 1989.

Weller, P., *Time for a change: reconfiguring religion, state and society*, London, T & T Clark, 2005.

Chapter 11

Campbell, A., *Rediscovering Pastoral Care* (2nd edn), London, Darton, Longman & Todd, 1986.

Carr, W., *Brief Encounters: Pastoral ministry through baptisms, weddings and funerals*, London, SPCK, 1994.

Carr, W., *Handbook of Pastoral Studies*, London, SPCK, 1997.

Harris, J., *Pastoral Theology: A black-church perspective*, Minneapolis, MN, Fortress Press, 1991.

Koenig, H. G., and Weaver, A. J., *Pastoral Care of Older Adults*, Minneapolis, MN, Fortress Press, 1998.

Patton, J., *Pastoral Care in Context: An Introduction to pastoral care*, Louisville, KY, Westminster John Knox, 1993.

Pembroke, N., *The Art of Listening: Dialogue, shame and pastoral care*, London, T. & T. Clark/Handsel, 2002.

Switzer, D. K., *Pastoral Care Emergencies*, Minneapolis, MN, Fortress Press, 2000.

Chapter 12

Coate, M., *Clergy Stress*, London, SPCK, 1989.

Claringbull, D., and Price, R., *Front Line Mission: Ministry in the market place*, London, Canterbury Press, 1994.

Edmonson, C., *Minister Love Thyself! Sustaining healthy ministry*, New York, Grove Press, 2000.

Foskett, J., and Lyall, D., *Helping the Helpers*, London, SPCK, 1988.

Helm, N., and Allin, P., (eds), *Finding Support in Ministry*, New York, Grove Press, 2002.

Walton, Graham E. H., and Ward, F., *Theological Reflection*, London, SCM, 2005.

Ward, F., *Lifelong Learning: Theological education and supervision*, London, SCM, 2005.

Chapter 13

Anderson, R. S., *Caregivers*, London, Jessica Kingsley, 2003.

The Archbishop's Council, *Mission-shaped Church: Church planting and fresh expressions of church in a changing context*, London, Church House Publishing, 2004.

Anderson, R.S., and Swinton, J., *Spiritual Caregiving as Secular Sacrament: A practical theology for professional transforming mission*, London, Jessica Kingsley, 2003.

Bosch, D.J., *Paradigm shifts in theology of mission*, Orbis Books, 1991.

Carr, W., *Ministry and the Media*, London, SPCK, 1990.

Chalke, S., *Faithworks: 2 stories of hope*, Eastbourne, Kingsway, 2001.

Claringbull, D., and Price, R., *Front Line Mission: Ministry in the market place*, London, Canterbury Press, 1994.

Clements, K., *Learning to Speak: The Church's voice in public affairs*, London, T. & T. Clark, 1995.

Costa, K., *God at Work: Living every day with purpose*, London, Continuum, 2007.

Fuller, J., and Vaughan, P., *Working for the Kingdom: The story of ministers in secular employment*, London, SPCK, 1996.

Green, L., *Urban Ministry and the Kingdom of God*, London, SPCK, 2003.

Legood, C., *Chaplaincy: The Church's sector ministries*, London, Cassell, 1999.